RAPID
Needs Analysis

**Tools, Worksheets, and
Job Aids to Help You:**

- **Determine in "Internet
  Time" if Analysis Is Needed**

- **Find and Analyze a
  Performance Problem Fast**

- **Recommend the Best
  Solution to Meet Business
  Needs**

ASTD

Linking People,
Learning & Performance

Susan Barksdale and Teri Lund

Ordering information: Books published by ASTD can be ordered by calling 800.628.2783 or 703.683.8100, or via the Website at www.astd.org.

Library of Congress Catalog Card Number: 2001117677

ISBN:1-56286-297-9

Contents

,

The demands of today's workplace have challenged the practice of needs analysis. Although there is concern and even controversy over whether taking the time to conduct needs analyses is worthwhile, we believe the practice is very important to workplace learning and performance. The question is not so much whether a needs analysis should be conducted, as how it can be completed quickly and accurately to meet business requirements.

A lengthy, time-consuming needs analysis is no longer practical and may not yield accurate information. Performance needs surface quickly and regularly in response to rapidly emerging business needs, and change at "Internet speed" is the rule rather than the exception. The good ol' days of taking two or more months to analyze an environment, work practices, and workers have come to an end. Many of the "old" needs analysis methods no longer work in today's business environment, and using them perpetuates the perception that our profession is always a step or two behind or, even worse, not responsive to our customers' needs.

Will conducting a needs analysis using a rapid approach compromise our professional standards, standards that many of us have been bound to for years? To the contrary, we believe that Rapid Needs Analysis does not compromise these standards, but rather adapts them to meet the requirements of today's workplace. Ultimately, this will help increase WLP's credibility and result in many more successes than failures.

To be sure, there is risk involved in conducting a Rapid Needs Analysis, because information that is gathered quickly and the resulting decisions may not always be 100% correct. But then again, the risk is greater if you use time-consuming, complex methods to analyze performance improvement needs that most likely will have changed by the time you complete your analysis.

We have worked in the WLP field for a combined total of 40 years and have spent much of that time focused on how to make the analysis of business and performance needs fast, efficient, and effective. Our experience with protracted analyses and identification of solutions that never made it to development because business needs changed during the analysis led us to experiment with different approaches to discovering needs. This experimentation resulted in the development of the Rapid Needs Analysis process.

We understand needs analysis from its theoretical roots, but this book also reflects what we have learned in "the school of hard knocks." It is the end result of our work over many years with numerous WLP clients to help them increase the quality of their deliverables and ensure their continued credible presence within the organization. We were encouraged by our clients and by those who have attended our public workshops to document this experience and provide a how-to book that would go beyond theory.

Think of this book as a guided tour of Rapid Needs Analysis led by two people who have been on the analysis front line and who have learned from their successes as well as their failures. We sincerely believe this book reflects what we have learned and will help you analyze business and performance needs to identify the best solutions possible.

Susan Barksdale and Teri Lund
August 2001

*R*apid Needs Analysis provides a practical framework to use in conducting an analysis of a performance problem quickly and efficiently. We describe the Rapid Needs Analysis process and provide methods and tools that you can use in almost every situation that requires analysis. Case studies in every chapter illustrate each step in the process and describe how other companies have approached the process.

This workbook will help you decide if an analysis is needed and, if so, how to get it done quickly. It shows you how to analyze the request for a performance solution and how to assess the current situation.

The workbook also addresses how to analyze the data gathered and determine the specifications for a solution. The use of technology is extremely important in gathering and analyzing the data you need to recommend solutions that are both appropriate and timely. We provide guidelines for reviewing the solution requirements with your business partners, gaining their commitment to the solution, and initiating the design and development (or procurement) process.

You can use only those parts of the book you need. For example, if you are in the midst of conducting an analysis, you can focus on the rapid data gathering methods identified in chapter 2—Step 2: Identifying the Current Situation. Or if you have already collected the data and need help analyzing it quickly and accurately, you can use the methods and tools outlined in chapter 3—Step 3: Analyzing the Data. Appendix A, at the end of this workbook, will help you quickly find the specific tools you need from among the many presented.

Rapid Needs Analysis provides the most up-to-date, proved analysis techniques; it makes specific methods, case examples, checklists, and other tools available for immediate application to your organization. This workbook will show you how to

- analyze the request to develop a performance solution or conduct an analysis
- identify performance expectations

- plan for the analysis
- identify the current situation using the most appropriate data collection tools
- analyze the data collected
- identify the performance gap
- evaluate the identified solution
- determine and validate specifications for the solution with stakeholders, subject matter experts, and solution designers
- gain approval for developing the solution
- gain commitment to solution development and implementation
- initiate the development of the solution by completing design documents and a development project plan
- transfer responsibility for development to the development project manager.

Target Audiences

WLP practitioners, including trainers, instructional designers, organizational development consultants, and human performance technologists, will find this workbook most valuable. Managers in a variety of industries who are interested in or responsible for the effectiveness of WLP interventions may also find this book useful. If your job involves improving human performance and you are interested in quickly analyzing performance improvement needs, then *Rapid Needs Analysis* is important reading for you.

Structure of the Book

This book consists of six chapters that correspond to the steps in the Rapid Needs Analysis process.

Step 1: Analyzing the Request

In step 1, you will analyze the request, which usually takes one of two forms (a business partner will say either "this is what we need" or "this is the problem"). You must determine why the request is being made, how urgent it is, and how it is linked to the business needs and the desired outcome.

Step 2: Identifying the Current Situation

Step 2 involves gathering data from the environment so you can determine how employees are performing currently, identify the causes of performance problems, and identify environmental barriers that are affecting performance. Chapter 2 introduces data collection methods and the best uses of technology.

Step 3: Analyzing the Data

In step 3, you will analyze the information you gathered in the previous step and then compare it with the desired outcomes identified by your business partners in step 1. The type of analysis you use will be linked to the type of data gathering you conducted in step 2 and the ways you will use the data.

Step 4: Determining Solution Specifications

Step 4 addresses how to determine the specifications for the solution identified in the previous step through face-to-face meetings or physical or virtual war rooms. Chapter 4 also discusses how to identify resources, costs, and risks.

Step 5: Gaining Commitment

In step 5, you will learn how to gain commitment to developing the solution from those involved. You will learn ways to sell the solution and its benefits to stakeholders, subject matter experts, solution developers, the managers and supervisors of participants, and the participants themselves.

Step 6: Initiating Development of the Solution

The last step in the Rapid Needs Assessment process is initiating development of the solution, which involves collaborating with the development team to create a design document and a development project plan. This concludes the analysis project manager's responsibility for the solution, and the development project manager takes over.

Appendixes

In addition to the six chapters relating to each step of the Rapid Needs Analysis process, this workbook contains an index of the tools presented, a glossary of Rapid Needs Analysis terms, and a listing of needs analysis references.

The ASTD Learning and Performance Workbook Series

Rapid Needs Analysis is the second book in the ASTD Learning and Performance Workbook Series, which is designed to provide WLP practitioners with a foundation for the practices that are at the core of our profession. Much like this book, each workbook consists of a practical, step-by-step process and useful tools. The first workbook, *Rapid Evaluation,* was published in May 2001, and future workbooks will address rapid strategic planning, rapid competency development, and rapid project management.

You can use these workbooks individually to focus on a specific WLP practice, or they can be used together to provide a comprehensive overview of the practices that are most important to WLP. In any event, we are certain that you will benefit from the concepts, practices, and tools presented in this workbook and that you will be able to apply them to your work.

Step 1: Analyzing the Request

You have received a request either to develop a performance solution or to determine why a performance problem exists. The first step in the Rapid Needs Analysis process is to analyze this request. *Solution* in this context means a system for resolving a performance problem; the solution may combine methods such as training, incentives, or process improvements. A solution encompasses an *intervention,* which is a specific event that is implemented to close a performance gap. *Performance problem* refers to performance that is not meeting expected outcomes or producing expected results.

If the request is to develop a specific solution, you must determine if there is a need to take a step back and look more closely at the proposed solution. Together with the customer, you should determine why the solution is needed and if the one proposed really is the best solution to meet the performance and business needs.

If the request is to determine why a performance problem exists, your job will be a bit easier, because the requester likely is already educated about the value of analysis and will be a cooperative partner in its completion. At the very least, the customer who makes such a request recognizes that a closer look needs to be taken at the problem and why it exists.

It is entirely possible that you are the one who becomes aware of the problem and brings it and the need for analysis to management's attention. If this is the case, you will need to actively market your analysis services.

Regardless of how the request is initiated, six key questions should be answered following the request:

1. What is the request, and why is it being made?

2. What is the urgency of the request?

3. What information needs to be collected and analyzed to design or procure the correct solution?

4. How closely is the request linked to the business?

5. What outcomes are expected, and are they clear?

6. What is the impact of the request on human resources?

If these questions are not answered up front and quickly, the potential exists for wasting your time in needless activities or getting bogged down in useless detail resulting in a protracted, rather than rapid, analysis. Knowing this information will help you position your response to the request and help you determine if an analysis really is needed. Even if the analysis is completed in an accelerated mode, it is a waste of time if unnecessary or ill timed.

At the end of step 1 you will know

- the information that needs to be gathered and how to get it quickly
- the information you have and how to validate it quickly
- how big the analysis is (the *scope*)
- who your customers are
- the expected outcomes for the solution
- the content of your Rapid Needs Analysis action plan.

Case Examples

Requests for needs analysis usually involve the need either to develop a specific solution or to identify the causes of a performance problem. The following case examples illustrate how WLP professionals handled each type of request.

Case Example 1

A financial institution with an emerging national presence operated in 12 western states, the result of a significant expansion in a relatively short period. In the past, the bank had enjoyed a solid reputation, and its financial success was built largely on its excellent customer service and competitive products. With the expansion, management wanted the bank's reputation and success to be consistent from state to state and employee to employee. The managers determined that the way to achieve this goal was to implement an electronic performance support system (EPSS) that would provide consistent, up-to-the-minute customer, product, and competitor information. The expected outcomes of the solution were to increase sales and profitability, decrease customer complaints, and increase employee satisfaction.

Management presented the WLP manager with a request for training to prepare employees to use the new system. The initial request involved developing the training after the system was developed. The manager, having experienced unsuccessful system conversions in the past, recognized an opportunity to sell the senior managers involved on the idea of basing the training on the system requirements, in effect developing the training as the system was being developed.

The WLP manager quickly validated the request with the project sponsors (one of whom was the requester) and determined that a rapid needs analysis was necessary so that the training could be developed along with the system. In fact, the results from the analysis were used in designing the EPSS. The WLP manager was able to sell the analysis because of the high cost of the system and the fact that if people were trained to use it correctly, productivity and sales would increase, errors would decrease, and customers and employees would be satisfied.

Case Example 2

The management of an electric utility with an international presence knew there was a problem with its supervisors. Deregulation, increased competition, union difficulties, reorganization, a high degree of leadership change, and lack of organizational communication resulted in enormous confusion and inaction. The supervisory group, largely promoted from the rank and file, did not have the supervisory skills needed to lead employees during the tremendous change from a local union shop to a highly dynamic international organization.

The senior management asked WLP management to provide more structure to the supervisory training program and to ensure that the supervisors were trained to handle current as well as anticipated future issues and problems. WLP was unsure about what was needed, how to set priorities for supervisory training, and where procedures needed to be clearly defined in this new environment.

The WLP manager validated with senior management that the supervisory program was an important short- and long-term operational issue and key to the organization's business and strategic success. Because the request for the analysis came from such a high level in the organization, the commitment for it was already present. However, it was extremely important that senior management saw that action was being taken

quickly to improve the business and its operations. Together they determined that an analysis would need to be detailed and to determine the training requirements regarding

- supervision of sales and customer service
- union leadership and contract obligations and maintenance of good relationships with the union
- environmental conditions for supervisors
- cultural norms and supervisory challenges
- safety requirements
- organizational understanding
- business strategy support
- deregulation and its effects on the business.

Step 1 Activities

Step 1 of the Rapid Needs Analysis process comprises 10 activities:

1. validating the request
2. determining the background information needed
3. identifying the business need for the analysis
4. identifying the expected outcomes for the solution
5. analyzing the risks involved in conducting the analysis
6. gaining commitment to conduct the analysis
7. clarifying the information needed from the analysis based on the type of request
8. determining the information you have and what you need
9. defining specific information
10. developing the Rapid Needs Analysis project plan.

This chapter explains each activity in detail and provides the tools you need to complete this step.

Validating the Request

Once you have received the request (or, as happens in some cases, after you have initiated the contact), it is your job to contact the requester to clarify what is being requested, to determine who and what is behind the request, and to assess its level of urgency. This information may be revealed automatically during the initial contact with the requester or may require a call back or short in-person meeting. It may require no meeting at all if you already are knowledgeable about the requester and the situation.

Let's assume that you need a brief telephone meeting with the requester because you are unfamiliar with the situation. In this meeting it is important that two things happen: 1) that you gather and validate as much information as possible about the request as quickly as possible, and 2) that you communicate parameters to the requester for what you will do as a result of the request.

The information you need to gather and validate from the requester includes the following:

- What is the request? What specifically are you being asked to do?

- What is the requester's role? Is the requester a sponsor, a stakeholder, a business partner, or someone other than the person who contacted you?

- What or who is driving the request? For example, is the requester grasping at straws to boost productivity or reduce costs or being forced to contact you because his or her manager thinks it is a good idea, or is there real commitment to solving a performance problem using the professional expertise you provide?

- What is the urgency of the request? When does the requester expect the analysis and solution to be completed? Is he or she aware of the time it will take to get to the finished product? If the request is extremely urgent, why? What has changed in the business that is making the performance problem critical? If the request is not urgent, then why is it being made? What is the risk of not responding to the request?

- What does the requester stand to gain or lose from the outcome of this request? Ultimately, what's in it for him or her to solve the performance problem? If the requester has no stake in the outcomes the solution is supposed to deliver, then it is doubtful that you will gain enough commitment to conduct an analysis, let alone develop a solution.

- Who will work with you to identify critical information, including business drivers, expected outcomes, available resources, and associated risks?

Table 1.1 provides more detail about the information you need regarding the request.

The parameters of your response to the request that should be communicated to the requester during this meeting include the following:

- An analysis most likely will be required if the request is to develop a solution. The analysis will help determine if the solution will meet business and performance needs through the desired outcomes.

- The analysis can be completed quickly—sometimes in as few as 10 days.

- The analysis will be done with help from the requester.

- Just because an analysis has been conducted does not mean that the solution identified by the requester will be the solution recommended.

- If the requested solution or performance problem identification is not urgent, is not linked to business needs, or lacks management commitment, there probably is no need to conduct an analysis or develop a solution.

- The work environment will be respected during the analysis, and as little disruption as possible will take place.

- Analysis is the first step of solution design, and gathering information will ensure effective and efficient design that will not need to be reworked.

Whether conducted in person or by telephone, this validation meeting is critical in establishing the need for and importance of the analysis and helps position the additional fact finding you will do in this step as a way to determine if an analysis will be conducted. Further detail on the information that you should communicate is listed in table 1.2.

Determining the Background Information Needed

The first activity in identifying the overall parameters of the project is gathering background information. You will need information about the following factors:

- how the problem links to the business
- the specific desired outcomes for the solution
- the resources needed for the analysis
- the risk involved in the project
- who needs to commit to the analysis.

Table 1.3 lists the important background information that you will gather at the beginning of the analysis and can be used in planning the project.

Table 1.1: Gathering and Validating Information

Information Needed	Rationale
What is the request?	To clarify what you are being asked to provide so you know how to respond. Perhaps the person is requesting a solution for which a program already exists, or he or she may be requesting analysis of a problem that is not a performance improvement problem. To clarify the breadth, depth, desired results, and immediacy of the request.
Who is requesting the solution or analysis of a performance problem?	To identify who, which often leads to why, is the critical thing to discover in this activity. You will also want to know what each person's level of authority and influence are so you will know if you have to go further up in the organization to sell the analysis and gain support. Is the requester the sponsor? If not, who is? Will the requester provide the funding for the analysis and the solution? To clarify the role and authority of the requester.
Who else is involved?	To determine who the other stakeholders are (assuming the requester is one), who your business partners are, and who your customers are. To determine who else has a significant role in this request.
What or who is behind the request?	To assess whether the request is being made due to a change in business drivers or some other organizational change or whether it is personality driven. This information will make a big difference in how you respond to and approach the analysis. To determine if there is a hidden agenda. To determine what is prompting the request and why.
What is the urgency of the request?	To determine why the request is being made now—what has changed in the business? To determine requester expectations for delivery of the solution. To determine the time frame of the request for the analysis and the design of the solution.
What will this person stand to gain or lose from solving the performance problem?	To determine why the request is being made and to begin to assess commitment to analyzing the performance problem. To identify the risk tolerance of the requester for a correct and incorrect solution (the lower the tolerance of risk, the greater the importance of analysis).
Who will work with you to identify critical information?	To make certain someone is available and responsible to help identify information needed.

Table 1.2: Points to Communicate During the Initial Contact

Point to Communicate	Rationale
Some form of analysis will most likely be required to complete the design or procure resources for a solution.	To let the requester know up front that you will analyze the need for the solution or cause of the performance problem.
The analysis will be completed quickly.	To assure the requester that you will not get trapped in "analysis paralysis."
The requester or his or her staff, or both, will be involved.	To prepare the requester for his or her involvement and the involvement of others involved in or affected by the solution.
As a result of the analysis, the solution that was requested may not be the solution recommended or may evolve to something else.	To prepare the requester for the possibility that you will recommend something other than what was requested.
If it is determined that the performance problem is not linked to business needs, is not urgent, or lacks management support, an analysis probably is not needed.	To inform the requester that it may not be prudent or a good use of time to conduct an analysis because you have already identified reasons for not developing the solution.

Table 1.3: Background Information Important to a Rapid Needs Analysis Project

Information Gathered	Rationale
How the problem links to the business	Validates and determines extent and breadth of the problem, which determine the number of resources you will need to research (e.g., smaller problem and breadth affect fewer employees).
Expected outcomes	Identifies the type of information regarding the performance problem and the solution parameters. For example, if one desired outcome is increased system capability, the solution must include a hands-on element.
Resources to assist in the analysis	You depend on others to help you gather information that is vital to an accurate analysis. Resources include human resource and customer information systems.
Risk assessment	The higher the risk of the solution being incomplete or "wrong," the more information must be gathered and the more detailed the analysis must be.
Commitment	The number of parties whose commitment is required corresponds to the length of time it takes to gain commitment. Consequently, the fewer reviewers needed, the better for a rapid analysis.

Identifying the Business Need for the Analysis

An important component of a needs analysis is linking the performance need to the organization's business drivers and business needs. A clear understanding of how the solution links to the business makes it possible for you to decrease steps or take shortcuts in the analysis and still ensure that the solution resulting from the analysis will meet its expected outcomes.

Business drivers are the external and internal factors that drive an organization's strategy and therefore its business and performance needs. External business drivers are outside of an organization's control and typically include the following:

- *Economic drivers* include upturns or downturns in the economy, embargoes or trade restrictions, and other economically driven situations.

- *Human resource drivers* include shortages of resources or of certain skills, union demands or contracts, and employee needs to balance family and work relationships.

- *Government drivers,* such as regulations or deregulation, force changes in competition or the environment as a whole.

- *Public perception drivers* involve the public's view of the organization. This view may be influenced by press coverage of an event or situation that arose outside of the organization's control.

- *Market or customer drivers* include increased competition or other changes in how the organization views the marketplace in which it competes, as well as changes in customer demographics, definition, and needs that place demands on products or necessitate changes in product design.

Internal business drivers are generated by internal decisions. Sometimes an internal business driver is a response to an external business driver. There typically is a stakeholder inside of the organization for this type of driver. Internal drivers include the following:

- *Technology drivers* are new innovations and technology that create opportunities or needs for changes in information keeping and processing.

- *Changes in system, process, or key policy drivers* change employee skill or behavior requirements.

- *Shareholder or financial drivers* include Wall Street or bank demands for higher profits or lower costs to which the organization must respond.

- *New product generation drivers* are market or customer changes that result in new or revised products or services to meet demand or need.

An organization identifies business needs, and corresponding objectives and strategies, to respond to business drivers. For example, if the business driver is increased competition, a business need may be to cut costs in other parts of the organization in order to reduce prices to the customer and undercut the competition.

The performance need defines what individual employees must achieve to address the business driver and support the corresponding business need. For example, if increasing market share was an identified business driver, a business need may be to sell more products to a customer within the product family. The performance need identified is to increase the sales staff's product knowledge and recognition of which products within the product family complement each other and are potential prospects for a particular customer base.

Performance needs usually drive a performance solution. The same performance needs define the value of the solution to the organization and justify the organization's investment in it. Performance needs are also referred to as "expected performance" or "expected outcomes."

By identifying and linking business drivers to performance needs, you will be able to show how the requested solution will address the performance needs, business needs, and ultimately the business drivers. If the solution will have no impact, then the question is, Why solve the problem?

You can use the grid provided in worksheet 1.1 to identify and link business drivers, business needs, and performance needs to the requested or potential solution. In column 1, identify the requested or potential solution. In column 2, identify the performance need that the solution will address. In column 3, align the performance need to the business need, and finally, in column 4, align the business need to the business driver that has created the need for the solution. Note whether the business driver is external or internal. We recommend identifying no more than three business drivers so that you can focus on those that are most important to the organization.

Specific examples of this process are provided in the worksheet. In the first example, there is alignment between the potential solution and the performance need, business need, and business driver. In the second example, there is a huge "disconnect" between the requested solution, performance need, business need, and business driver. The solution request was a communication course to enable product engineers to communicate technical changes to marketing and manufacturing. Because of the shortage of highly skilled and experienced engineers, the company cannot replace retiring engineers with external resources. So the communication course is part, but not all, of the solution, and it will not be successful without technical knowledge and skills.

Next, you should review and validate with the requester your findings about the alignment of the business drivers, business needs, and performance needs. If there is no relationship between the driver and the solution (or only a loose relationship), then the solution may not be the right one. This discussion is critical to arriving at the decision to recommend the analysis.

Identifying the Expected Outcomes for the Solution

Now that you have identified the business drivers and linked them to the requested solution, you will need to identify the expected outcomes of the solution. This is another, and final, way to validate the need for the solution and therefore the need for the analysis.

To save time, we recommend that you identify outcomes at the same time that you validate the business need for the solution. Again, this meeting can be accomplished either in person or by phone and should take at most one hour, providing the content to be discussed during the meeting is sent in advance to the people attending.

During this meeting you should identify what the requester hopes to accomplish through the performance solution. What does he or she want the audience to do as a result of the solution? Examples of outcomes are "to sell more product," "to reduce scrap," "to decrease design time," or "to decrease the time to market."

Worksheet 1.1: Aligning the Requested or Potential Solution with the Performance Need, Business Need, and Business Driver

1 Requested or Potential Solution	2 Performance Need	3 Business Need	4 Business Driver
Electronic performance support system that provides customer information, product knowledge, sales prompts, and up-to-date competitor product information (Potential solution)	Increased knowledge of competitors' and one's own products Increased knowledge about how to sell against competition	To increase presence in market; key competitors are offering products in new marketplaces on ongoing basis	Loss of market share (competition) (external driver)
External one-week course to address communication issues among product engineers (Requested solution based on personality problems among product engineers)	Provide identified high-potential employees with the knowledge and skills needed to replace retiring engineers Transfer retiring engineer knowledge base to selected employees in a logical and organized way	As product engineers are retiring, prepare for future by identifying high-potential employees and investing in their development	Labor market shortage (human resources) (external driver)

The requester may identify a multitude of desired outcomes that, on closer examination, are overlapping or redundant. We recommend distilling these outcomes to an important few (no more than five), which you can do after the meeting. These outcomes will provide the parameters for what you will explore during the analysis and ultimately will be used to identify the objectives and measures for the solution itself.

The outcomes identified must be

- realistic—Are they sound? Do they make sense?

- business related—Are they related to the business needs and ultimately business drivers?

- measurable—Can they be measured so the solution's success can be evaluated?

- achievable—Are they achievable given the current business environment?

If the requester is not able to identify outcomes, why not? Is the business need still unclear? Is the requested or potential solution off track? Is the problem not really a performance problem? If so, the analysis of the requested solution should not take place.

Worksheet 1.2 contains a grid that can be used to work through the identification of outcomes with the requester. It should look familiar, because it has all of the elements of worksheet 1.1, but the columns are reversed to start with the business driver and work back to the outcomes. Identifying outcomes in this way will help you ensure they are aligned with the business goals. In columns 1, 2, and 3, identify the business drivers, business needs, and performance needs linked to your requested or potential solution (column 4). Then identify the expected outcomes from the solution in column 5. The first example from worksheet 1.1 is used to illustrate this process.

Analyzing the Risks Involved in Conducting the Analysis

At this point you should have the information you need to determine if you will recommend conducting a needs analysis. During the risk analysis, you will need to answer questions such as the following: What

---

Worksheet 1.2: Outcomes Identification Worksheet

1 Business Driver	2 Business Need	3 Performance Need	4 Requested or Potential Solution	5 Outcomes
Loss of market share (competition) (external driver)	To increase presence in market; key competitors are offering products in new marketplaces on ongoing basis	Increased knowledge of competitors' and one's own products Increased knowledge about how to sell against competition	Electronic performance support system that provides customer information, product knowledge, sales prompts, and up-to-date competitor product information	To be able to sell against competitors' products To answer customer questions about competitors' products To use customer information during the sales call To increase customer product penetration To increase customer retention To reduce customer product complaints and returns

---

will happen if the performance problem is not solved? Will there be any impact at all on the business? If there is no impact on the business, then why solve the problem? What is the risk involved in not providing a solution to the problem?

Worksheet 1.3 can help you make your decision. The risk factors involved in conducting the analysis, which you investigated earlier in step 1, are listed in the left-hand column. In the right-hand column, note your assessment of each risk factor. When you have completed this worksheet, you will have identified potential risks that exist in conducting a Rapid Needs Analysis and should know if an analysis is warranted. If you identify more than three or four risk factors, you may want to reconsider the project as a candidate for Rapid Needs Analysis. You will also know what might happen if you do not do an analysis or agree to the requester's initial request.

Gaining Commitment to Conduct the Analysis

Once you have made the decision to recommend a needs analysis to your requesters, you must gain their commitment to complete it. If you have gathered the information identified thus far in step 1, you should have no surprises.

Before you ask for commitment to the analysis, it is helpful to take a quick inventory of the information you have gathered on the request up to this point. Worksheet 1.4 is provided to ensure that you have documented this information and to prompt you to obtain any that is missing before asking for commitment. The information required at this point is listed in the left-hand column. In the middle column you should note whether or not you have gathered the information, and in the right-hand column you should note if more information is needed before you ask for commitment to conduct the analysis.

You should now have a good feel for whether you will have the support needed from management to conduct the analysis and eventually design and develop the solution. If you encounter resistance at this point, most likely you will have to gather additional information to find out why. Perhaps some information was missing from your initial analysis of the request or a key person was missing from the meetings. Some issues to consider if you run into resistance include the following:

- Identify who has the most to gain or lose from the study. How will the results affect them; how will they benefit from the study?

- Find out not only who does not agree with conducting the analysis, but why. Become knowledgeable about time and money constraints and the politics surrounding the situation.

- Articulate the performance need in business terms, and state the benefits of the analysis as related to business results. Selling the need for the analysis by emphasizing its benefits is particularly effective if done from the client's perspective—what's in it for them to have the analysis completed?

- Being clear about the consequences of not conducting an analysis will help you gain commitment to it. Consequences may include spending money on the wrong performance intervention, developing a solution that is outmoded in the current environment, or alienating the audience with irrelevant training.

Although the commitment you receive at this point is verbal, we recommend that you get written agreement, or "signoff," to conduct the analysis when you present the project plan to the requester, sponsor, and stakeholders.

It is entirely possible that you will decide not to conduct the analysis. If this is the case, it is your responsibility to contact the requester and those involved in the process and to be as candid as possible about why you made that decision. Worksheet 1.3 should be helpful to you in explaining these reasons.

Clarifying the Information Needed from the Analysis Based on the Type of Request

At this point it is helpful to clarify the type of information that is needed from the analysis based on the type of request that has been made. This will help target the data collection to validate the request and to meet the performance gap.

The following are the most frequent types of solution requests that WLP professionals receive:

- a new process or process change. The requester typically asks for your help in redesigning a process, such as streamlining an order process or decreasing the time it takes to design a new product before it goes to manufacturing, or in providing training or performance support for the redesign.

Worksheet 1.3: Risk Analysis Worksheet

Risk Factor	Your Assessment
Reasons for the request	
Commitment of sponsors	
Clarity of business drivers	
Level of urgency	
Alignment of proposed or potential solution with business need	
Alignment of proposed or potential solution with expected outcomes	
Business linkage	
Availability of information needed	
Availability of funding	
Availability of human resources required	
Potential environmental barriers to solution's success	
Stability of environment (i.e., will the environment change before the solution can be implemented?)	
Level of commitment needed from those who will be involved in providing information for the analysis	
Other risk factors	

Worksheet 1.4: Background Information Inventory

Information Required	Information Gathered?		More Information Needed?	
	Yes	No	Yes	No
Identity of the requester	❏	❏	❏	❏
Identity of the sponsors	❏	❏	❏	❏
Identity of other key players who have an interest in the performance problem	❏	❏	❏	❏
General description of the targeted audience	❏	❏	❏	❏
Description of the performance improvement need as identified by the requester	❏	❏	❏	❏
Determination of whether or not the problem really is a performance problem	❏	❏	❏	❏
Project scope	❏	❏	❏	❏
Project urgency	❏	❏	❏	❏
Potential project risks	❏	❏	❏	❏
Expected outcomes for the solution	❏	❏	❏	❏

- an identified skill need. The requester says, "We have identified a need for employees to have the ability to . . . ." The requester is specific about what type of proficiency is needed, and your job is to determine how to develop the proficiency.

- an identified knowledge need. The requester has identified a knowledge gap and requests that you develop employees' "information base." For example, the employee needs to "recall" or "translate" information. You need to determine how to transfer the knowledge to the employee in a way that can be applied back on the job.

- a new system or system change. The requester asks you to provide performance support for a new system or a system change. A new system typically involves comprehensive change (including process changes, skill building, and knowledge acquisition), and it also has to be completed in a short time, which is why this type of request is included in the Rapid Needs Analysis process.

- a defined performance gap. The requester defines the performance gap but not whether it is a specific skill or knowledge deficiency (or

some combination). For this type of request, you must identify what the audience needs to meet the desired performance before you can develop a solution or intervention.

- a predefined solution or intervention. The requester has the "fix" in mind, such as "We need Company XYZ's sales training course" or "We need team building [or leadership or another kind of] training." In this case you first need to validate the performance problem and desired outcomes, and then you need to determine if the requester's solution is the correct one—all without creating a political nightmare!

- a job aid. The requester makes a specific request for assistance with a specific job function or set of information in a very "job friendly" presentation. The information needed is reasonably clear, and your job is to determine the format for presentation or delivery.

- unidentified performance gap—defined business need. The business need has been identified (e.g., sales need to increase, errors need to decrease, customer complaints need to be resolved), but the how, what, and who may not be clearly defined.

Table 1.4 lists the most frequent types of requests and the information you will need to gather to respond to the request and provide specifications for design, development, purchase, and implementation. Also listed in this table are data gathering and other activities that should be included in the project plan.

To validate that you have indeed identified the information needed, compare the request and the information needed against the desired outcomes (see worksheet 1.2) and determine if there is alignment. An example of how to do this is provided in worksheet 1.5, which can help you identify the information you think

Table 1.4: Clarifying the Information Needed from the Analysis Based on the Type of Request		
Type of Request	**Information Needed from Analysis**	**Potential Activities for Gathering Information**
New process or process change	What the process is (e.g., step outline, outputs) Who will be affected by the change and how A comparison of the old environment with the new environment How the process change will be implemented Documentation or supporting materials that define the new process (and old process if it is a change) Identification of environmental issues Data to support performance problem Listing of previous programs Audience information	Focus groups and interviews (minimum one week for script and interview development and facilitation) to assess perspectives, expectations, and so forth Observations of current environment to assess change (minimum three days) Review of documentation (minimum two days)
Identified skill need	Definition of the skill (e.g., what is "overcomes resistance"?) Definition of the current skill level (or if skill even exists in desired populations) Definition of desired skill outputs Identification of environmental issues Data to support performance problem Listing of previous programs Audience information	Interviews of "skill experts" to define skill and expected outputs as well as required foundational skills (minimum one week for script and interview development and facilitation) Focus groups or observations to gain input on skill level or foundation requirements (minimum one week)
Identified knowledge need	Definition of the knowledge (e.g., what is "understands the parts specification process"?) Definition of the current knowledge level (or if knowledge even exists in desired populations) Definition of desired knowledge outputs Identification of environmental issues Data to support performance problem Listing of previous programs Audience information	Interview "knowledge experts" to define knowledge and expected outputs as well as required foundational knowledge (minimum one week for script and interview development and facilitation) Focus groups or observations to gain input on knowledge level or foundation requirements (minimum one week)

Table 1.4: Clarifying the Information Needed from the Analysis Based on the Type of Request (continued)

Type of Request	Information Needed from Analysis	Potential Activities for Gathering Information
New system or system change	System specifications Projection of performance needs (skill and knowledge) Projection of process changes Assessment of job impact Identification of environmental issues Data to support performance problem Listing of previous programs Audience information	Review of documentation (specifications and projections) (minimum three days) Observations or focus groups (minimum one week)
Defined performance gap	Assessment of current environment against desired outcomes to identify skill or knowledge gap Identification of environmental issues Data to support performance problem Listing of previous programs Audience information	Focus groups or interviews to gain perception of performance need and resistance to gap identification or change (minimum one week) Observations to validate gap and determine skill or knowledge requirements (minimum two weeks)
Predefined solution or intervention	Validation of request against audience perception Identification of environmental issues Data to support performance problem Listing of previous programs Audience information	Focus groups or interviews (minimum one week)
Job aid	Review of documentation or information needed Audience preferences for design Identification of environmental issues Data to support performance problem Listing of previous programs Audience information	Documentation review (minimum one day) Interviews or focus groups (minimum one week)
Unidentified performance gap—defined business need	Organization information Identification of best practice information Identification of environmental issues Data to support performance problem Listing of previous programs Audience information	Literature search (minimum two days) Organizational background research (minimum two days) Survey (optional) (minimum two weeks) Focus groups (minimum one week) Observations (minimum three days)

is needed to support the expected outcomes. If, through the analysis, you have a good understanding of the kinds of customer problems that typically arise and the appropriate action and response for each (left-hand column), then you will be able to build a solution (right-hand column) to ensure that customer need is analyzed and appropriate action is taken (middle column).

In the first entry in worksheet 1.5, the information identified as needed from the analysis and the desired outcomes are not in alignment. The information needed was knowledge acquisition, but the outcomes indicate a need for skill building (analysis is a skill, but a foundation for analysis is knowledge of the information or steps undertaken when analyzing). In this situation, you would need to go back to the requester and validate the outcomes against the request with questions such as the following:

1. Do you want the audience to analyze the information (skill), or do you want them to understand the analysis process (knowledge)?

2. Do you want them to probe more deeply into customer problems (skill), or do you want them to classify the problems into specific categories for escalation to a higher-level employee or supervisor (knowledge)?

3. Do you want them to interpret data (knowledge) or test and examine data (skill)?

In the second example in worksheet 1.5, the information does align with outcomes. The information needed was for a process, and the outcomes are for employees to use a specific process.

Determining the Information You Have and What You Need

You need to collect information to identify the current situation. Some of this information you already may have from analyzing the request, and some of it you will need to collect by going out to the environment. This may be as easy as sending an email message to one of your identified resources, or it can be as complex as getting management approval to review a confidential report that contains pertinent organizational information. Keep in mind that the amount of information gathered will affect the amount of analysis required and, ultimately, the amount of time it takes to complete the next step in the process. Key to rapid analysis is focusing on the information most critical to determining the performance problem and getting to the "right" solution.

Worksheet 1.6 can help you organize this activity. It lists the information most typically needed to identify the current situation. You can use this worksheet to determine what information you already have and what you need to collect.

Worksheet 1.5: Validating the Information Needed from the Analysis

Information Needed	Expected Outcome	In Alignment?
Understanding of customer problem and identification of appropriate response	Customer need is analyzed and appropriate action is taken	No
Documentation for the new process Perspective of the audience regarding the changes the new process will create Analysis of the current environment against the new environment	Ensure that new procurement or supply request process is followed by all departments Reduce number of suppliers by centralizing procurement	Yes

Worksheet 1.6: Information Collection Needs

Type of Information Needed	Have Information	Need Information	Do Not Need Information
Organizational information: • strategic plans • mission statements • goals and objectives • organization charts • descriptions of major initiatives • other			
Best practice information: • leaders in the industry (what are their practices, and why are these practices seen as best in class?) • leaders in developing state-of-the-art performance solutions • other			
Past and current programs that address identified performance problem: • training • processes • systems • other initiatives			
Audience information: • who • how many • location • education level • experience level • current job knowledge • current job skills • current job performance • current job attitudes • physical conditions of the work area • nature and extent of supervision • position descriptions • others who influence or support the targeted audience • performance plans • other			
Environmental issues: • constraints • politics • cultural factors • economic factors • other			

(continued next page)

Worksheet 1.6: Information Collection Needs (continued)

Type of Information Needed	Have Information	Need Information	Do Not Need Information
Data to support performance problem and expected outcomes: • performance results • customer feedback • lost revenue • increased costs • attrition rates • other			

Defining Specific Information

In table 1.5 the information you most likely will gather for a needs analysis is presented with questions you should pose as you

- gather research information (ask yourself)
- conduct interviews or focus groups (ask others)
- design or implement surveys (ask yourself and others)
- review documentation or background information (ask yourself and others).

The type of information is accompanied by the questions that will help you define the specific information you need.

Developing the Rapid Needs Analysis Project Plan

One last activity remains in analyzing the request: developing the needs analysis project plan. A project plan is necessary in communicating analysis responsibilities, timelines, and deliverables. Developing a written project plan is critical in Rapid Needs Analysis because of the amount of information that has to be collected and processed in a short period of time and the variety of people who will help collect it.

Tool 1.1 lists the major milestones, time frames, and deliverables that are part of a Rapid Needs Analysis project. You can enter the content of this plan into your project planning software program to expedite this planning process.

Table 1.5: Defining Specific Information

Information to Gather	Question or Probe
Organizational information	How would the intervention or solution support the organization's strategy or initiative? Is this type of request in alignment with the organization's goals and objectives? What is the "span of influence" of this request (who would be affected, and how)? Does or will the request support a major initiative, or is it in conflict with a major initiative? How would the organization benefit if the requested solution or intervention is successful? How would you know?

Table 1.5: Defining Specific Information (continued)

Information to Gather	Question or Probe
Best practices information	Who is seen as a best practice organization for this type of request? Why? What makes it a best practices organization?
	How is that organization different from yours? How is it the same?
	What would have to change within your organization to mirror or exceed the best practices organization? How would this change occur?
	What constraints currently exist in your organization that may limit its ability to become a best practices organization? Why do these constraints exist?
Past and current programs that address identified performance problem	What past or current programs address the request?
	What past or current programs do you see as a foundation (or knowledge or skill builder) that support but do not meet the request? Why or how?
	What percentage of the audience has participated in past or current programs?
	What is not working or disliked about past or current programs?
	What is working well or liked about past or current programs?
	How do past or current programs relate to this request?
Audience information	What is the audience's perception of the request (e.g., problem, need, change)?
	Is there resistance, and if so, what is it?
	What does the audience see as the request?
	What are the audience requirements or preferences that may influence the request (e.g., no travel, face-to-face interaction)?
	What is a motivator for the audience to participate and implement the change that will result from the request?
	What are the audience demographics?
	What constraints exist for the audience?
Environmental issues	What constraints exist in the environment that might limit the success of the request?
	What is the environment?
	Who has control over the environment, and what is their perception of the request?
	How will the environment affect the request? What is the relationship of the environment to the request?
	How has the environment influenced the need for the request?
Data to support performance problem and expected outcomes	Is the request valid?
	How does the performance information (perceived or actual) support or contradict the request?
	Would these outcomes occur if the request were implemented? How would you know?
	How would you know if the request were successful?
	How would you know if the request were unsuccessful?

Tool 1.1: Prototype of a Rapid Needs Analysis Project Plan

Step 1: Analyzing the Request

Major Milestones
Validate the request
Determine what background information is needed
Identify the business need for the analysis
Identify the expected outcomes for the solution
Analyze the risks involved in conducting the analysis
Gain commitment to conduct the analysis
Clarify information needed from the analysis based on the type of request
Determine what information you have and what you need
Define specific information
Develop the Rapid Needs Analysis project plan

Time frame
1–2 days

Deliverables
Recommendation to conduct (or not conduct) the analysis
List of information to be gathered and how it will be gathered
Outcomes expected from the solution
Rapid Needs Analysis project plan

Step 2: Identifying the Current Situation

Major Milestones
Locate the needed information
Determine the data collection methods
Develop the instruments to gather the information
Test the data gathering instruments
Gather the identified information
Identify gaps and errors in the information
Collect additional information if needed

Time frame
6–10 days (depending on the methods used and types of instruments developed)

Deliverables
List of information to be gathered and data collection methods
Data collection instruments
Data regarding current situation

Tool 1.1: Prototype of a Rapid Needs Analysis Project Plan (continued)

Step 3: Analyzing the Data

Major Milestones
Plan the data analysis
Choose the type of analysis
Identify data bias
Analyze the data
Interpret the results
Align results with business drivers and business needs
Identify the performance gap
Evaluate the identified solution
Identify performance measures linked to expected outcomes
Validate the identified solution with the requester, sponsor, and stakeholder

Time frame
2–6 days (depending on how the data are analyzed)

Deliverables
Short report to document analysis findings

Step 4: Determining Solution Specifications

Major Milestones
Identify who will be involved in determining specifications
Communicate purpose, roles, and responsibilities
Discuss needs analysis findings
Determine the specifications
Finalize and validate the specifications
Identify resources needed to develop and implement the solution
Identify the costs associated with the solution
Identify the risks versus the benefits of the solution
Gain sponsor approval to proceed with developing the solution

Time frame
2–4 days

Deliverables
Detailed specifications for the solution

Step 5: Gaining Commitment

Major Milestones
Identify who needs to commit to the solution and why
Sell the benefits of their involvement

Time frame
1–2 days

(continued next page)

Tool 1.1: Prototype of a Rapid Needs Analysis Project Plan (continued)

Deliverables
Commitment to design, develop, and implement the solution

Step 6: Initiating Development of the Solution

Major Milestones
Create a design document for the solution
Create a development project plan
Transfer responsibility for solution development

Time frame
3–6 days

Deliverables
Solution design document
Development project plan

Chapter Summary

In this chapter, the first step of the Rapid Needs Analysis process was introduced and discussed. Case examples were presented that illustrate how two companies initiated the request for an analysis in very different ways. How to respond to the requester was addressed, along with how to gather pertinent information so you can analyze the request. The importance of determining the business need for the requested solution and outcomes, analyzing the risk of conducting the analysis, and making a decision whether to recommend an analysis was also addressed. Gaining commitment to conduct the analysis and clarifying the information needed from the analysis based on the request were also introduced, as were determining what information you have and what needs to be collected and how to define specific information needs. Finally, a Rapid Needs Analysis project plan prototype was provided.

Although on the surface step 1 may seem to contain a lot of detail and to require a lot of time, it can be completed very quickly. Think of it as insurance against spending more time conducting an analysis that is not needed or developing a wrong or unneeded solution.

Discussion Questions

The following questions are provided to help you apply what you learned in this chapter:

- What types of requests are you most likely to receive for developing a solution or analyzing a performance problem?

- Why is it important to validate or understand why the request is being made?

  _____

  _____

- What type of information is critical to gather during the initial request?

  _____

  _____

- What is important for you to communicate up front about the request?

  _____

  _____

- After you have validated the request, what additional information do you need to gather?

  _____

  _____

- Why is it so important to determine the business need for the request? How does determining the business need support completing a Rapid Needs Analysis that will provide results?

  _____

  _____

- What is one business driver that is affecting your organization today?

  _____

  _____

- What are expected outcomes, and what is the purpose in defining them in this step of the process? Why are they important in this first step?

  _____

  _____

- What is the purpose of conducting a risk analysis in this step, and what is the outcome of the risk analysis?

  _____

  _____

- What is one reason you may not gain commitment to conduct an analysis, and how could you overcome the resistance?

  _____

  _____

- Why is it important to clarify the information you need to collect based on the type of request at this point?

  _____

  _____

- Why do you need to define the specific information needed at this point?

- What is the value of completing a project plan for a Rapid Needs Analysis project?

2

Step 2: Identifying the Current Situation

Once you have analyzed the request to develop a specific solution or to identify a performance problem and you have determined that an analysis is needed, the next step in the Rapid Needs Analysis process is to identify the current situation. You must quickly gather information about what is happening within the organization, how the target audience is currently performing, the environmental barriers that need to be overcome, and the causes of performance problems.

During this step you will gather information about

- the organization
- best practices being applied to similar problems in other organizations
- existing training programs, processes, or other initiatives currently being used to remedy the performance problem
- the audience
- environmental issues.

At the end of step 2 you will have the information you will need to

- identify the environmental barriers that need to be addressed
- assess how employees are performing today
- spot the causes of performance problems.

This information will be used later in the Rapid Needs Analysis process to determine the gap between expected performance and current performance and to begin to develop the specifications for a solution.

Case Examples

Case examples that illustrate how to identify the current situation are provided throughout this chapter.

Step 2 Activities

There are seven activities to complete in step 2 of the Rapid Needs Analysis process:

1. locating the needed information
2. determining the data collection methods
3. developing the instruments to gather the information
4. testing the data gathering instruments
5. gathering the information
6. identifying gaps and errors in the information collected
7. collecting additional information if needed.

This chapter explains each activity in detail and provides the tools you need to complete this step.

Locating the Needed Information

The first activity in step 2 is identifying where the information you need is located and who can assist in collecting it. Some of the information will be on systems such as human resource information systems (HRIS), customer information systems, and statistical application programs, and you need simply to get access to it or to identify a contact to help you get it. Information such as audience size and location, past and current audience training, and customer feedback typically is on these systems. Other pieces of information can be gathered only from people such as the requester or sponsor, who may have pertinent organizational information known only to them. Certainly you will need to collect much of the audience information from the audience itself.

Worksheet 2.1 can help you identify where the information you need is located or who has it. Transfer the needed information you identified in worksheet 1.6 to the left-hand column of worksheet 2.1 under the corresponding category (organizational information, best practice information, past and current programs that address identified performance problem, audience information, environmental issues, and data to support performance problem and solution outcomes). Next, in the middle column, identify where the information is located or who has it. Finally, in the right-hand column, determine the availability of the information and note how easy or difficult it will be to gather. If you think you will have trouble gathering the information, state how you plan to work around this difficulty. Examples of how to complete the worksheet are provided.

Determining the Data Collection Methods

After you have determined what information you need to gather to identify the current situation and where or from whom to gather it, the next activity is to determine what method you will use to collect it. In addition to contacting specific people who can quickly provide the information you need, we have found the following six methods of data collection to be the most efficient and effective to use in Rapid Needs Analysis:

- online surveys
- electronic focus groups
- best practices literature searches
- job mapping
- observations
- telephone interviews.

Online Surveys

Online surveys are much like paper-based surveys except that they are distributed and collected electronically either through a Website or via email. They are useful information gathering tools because they reach a large and geographically dispersed audience and, if anonymity can be assured, usually result in a high rate of return. They are most appropriate for collecting information about the level of knowledge and skill the audience currently possesses, their confidence level in using their knowledge and skills, and their opinions and beliefs about what they need to do their jobs better.

Online surveys can shave weeks off the time it takes to conduct a needs analysis. You can send the survey to many people instantly through mail lists and other means of easy access. In addition, other database management systems can help you sort and analyze electronic survey responses.

Although online surveys are easy to distribute, complete, and return, with the amount of information being pushed to employees via email, surveys can easily be overlooked. So it is critical for your survey to stand out. Some organizations have offered employees incentives to complete surveys to make certain they get a response rate that will ensure a high confidence level.

Assuring the confidentiality of responses is another issue with online surveys; it can be guaranteed only if you control who has access to the data. Confidentiality is an important aspect of all employee surveys. If respondents do not believe the online survey is being controlled in a way that ensures confidentiality, they might not provide honest responses. You will need to work with your information services provider to ensure that the server (and the data stored on it) is secure.

Case Example: Online Survey

A well-known manufacturer of computer components used online surveys to gather information from a worldwide audience of resellers who relied on the organization to provide technical training to help them meet their sales and service needs. Using this method the survey was distributed and collected in one week.

Electronic Focus Groups

The time it takes to conduct in-person focus groups is not compatible with the Rapid Needs Analysis process. Although focus groups are a highly reliable method of gathering data, they are expensive and time intensive and often exclude people who are located away from the site. Using Web technology (much like interactive chat rooms), however, groups of employees, managers, and supervisors can be questioned and respond simultaneously. Everything written is seen by everyone at the same time, and verbatim recording is possible. Such focus groups can also have audio hookup, so that everything said is heard as well. The use of satellite technology often is more realistic than Web technology in conducting focus groups and is often available in hotels and other public places.

Focus groups are structured meetings that use a predeveloped script to obtain specific information for analyzing workplace learning and performance needs. The information gathered in a group setting is often richer than that obtained from surveys or individual interviews because the facilitator can probe responses more deeply. Focus groups are an excellent way to gather subjective information that can then be used to validate information collected through other methods.

The objective of a focus group is to gain information through a group interview. A focus group is an interview, not a problem-solving session or decision-making group, and it is important that participants understand this when they are chosen to participate. The participants hear each other's responses and make additional comments beyond their own original responses. The objective is to get high-quality data in a social context where people can consider

Worksheet 2.1 Locating the Needed Information

Information Needed	Where Located or Who Has Information	Availability of Information (or Plan for Getting It)
Organizational information: Descriptions of major initiatives	On various managerial reports—Project sponsor	Information available through sponsor who has a need to control the information. She is hard to pin down for telephone meeting, so will email request including benefits for the project and to her.
Best practice information: Industry leaders	Websites for industry trade groups	Readily available via Internet
Past and current programs that address identified performance problem: Training programs	Resides on training Website and with training coordinator	Website is secure and training coordinator is resistant to the needs analysis; must contact project sponsor to assist in getting the materials.
Audience information: Job knowledge	Target audience	Not known—must get from them
Environmental issues: Constraints	Managers and supervisors of target audience Target audience	Not known—must get from them
Data to support performance problem and expected outcomes: Customer feedback	Customer information system	Readily available

their own views in relation to the views of others. Neither consensus nor disagreement is necessary in the focus group.

Focus groups can be difficult to lead, even in electronic formats. They do not always promote synergy or result in the information desired. People and politics can hinder the gathering of useful information, and the process can deteriorate, resulting in confusion and conflict. An expert focus group facilitator is a necessity. Another downside to electronic focus groups is the expense of the systems used to conduct them and the advanced technical know-how needed to pull it off.

Case Example: Electronic Focus Group

The management of a call center within an international funds management company determined the need to develop a new electronic performance support system (EPSS) to replace several paper-based manuals that contained call-handling procedures, including a process for handling irate callers and call escalation. One method used to identify the content needed for the EPSS was an electronic focus group with the center managers, who were located around the world and who rarely were in the same place at the same time. The focus group was completed in one hour, and a transcript of the session was provided immediately following the event.

Best Practices Literature Searches

Best practices literature searches provide information about how other organizations with similar performance problems or needs have solved them and about industry trends. The Internet is extremely valuable in this type of search. There are several good search engines, such as Yahoo and Excite!, and databases such as ERIC. Organizations such as the American Society of Training and Development, Softbank Institute, and the International Society for Performance Improvement also have databases with search capability offered through Websites.

Case Example: Best Practices Literature Search

The education and training department of a nationally based insurance company was shifting from networked computer-based training to Internet-based "e-learning" and needed to research the training that would be needed to support this major change. As part of identifying the current situation, the project leader conducted a best practices literature search to see how other organizations handled this type of transition. The search included general search engines, WLP industry Websites and databases, competitor Websites, and relevant business journals. This search was completed in 1.5 days.

Job Mapping

Job mapping is a thorough walk-through of what employees do in their jobs. Its purpose is to identify the knowledge and skills required on the job, expected performance results, and barriers to doing the job. Job mapping, if set up correctly, can take the place of a traditional job or task analysis, in which the analyst observes and questions individual employees while they are doing the job. The traditional analysis can be one of the most time-consuming aspects of conducting a needs analysis.

Job mapping is conducted with a group of employees in the same job. If several different jobs make up the targeted audience, then you will need to map each job in a separate group. The goal of job mapping is to understand the details of what is done in each job, how it is done, when it is done, and who (or what) else might be involved in getting it done.

You can complete this method of data gathering quickly, but the amount of time it will take is highly dependent on the number of jobs performed by the target audience. Under normal circumstances, it takes approximately one-half to one day to map one job with a group of about 12 participants. So, if your audience performs three different jobs, it may take as many as nine hours to complete the mapping. It is not necessary to include every audience member in job mapping; you can use a sample of the audience that will give the level of confidence you want the data to provide. Job mapping can be completed in less than two thirds of the time it takes to conduct a job or task analysis and will provide the same type of information at the same level of quality.

Case Example: Job Mapping

The training department in a worldwide computer components company used job mapping to help identify the knowledge and skills needed for employees who assisted customers over their telephone help line and Website. Specifically, the job mapping helped identify the types of situations these employees encountered with customers, the processes and tools employees used to do their jobs, and the barriers to getting the job done as expected. There were three different jobs represented in the target audience, and the job mapping took nine hours to complete over 1.5 days.

Observations

Observations of tasks, processes, and service and product delivery within the workplace can help you determine skill and knowledge gaps as well as environmental flaws. Observations allow you to make inferences about the work climate, supervision, tools, accessibility of job aids, workflow, employees, and work patterns. They also allow you to familiarize yourself with the type of job you are analyzing by "experiencing" the environment firsthand.

Ideally, observations should be completed before developing interview questions and focus group guides. Observing the environment and individual workers is a good way for you to orient yourself to the analysis of performance problems.

Traditionally, observations are a costly method of gathering information because they are time and labor intensive. In Rapid Needs Analysis, observations usually are used in combination with other methods to gather general information about the work conditions and employee performance or as a way to validate the information gathered.

Case Example: Observations

A major retailer of athletic apparel and equipment faced problems in its central distribution center. Management requested that the training department analyze what was happening in the center and come up with a training plan. Once the training department determined that an analysis would be conducted, a consultant assigned to the project conducted a general observation of the center in one hour and spent another four hours observing employees in the four different positions in the center. This observation helped the consultant quickly understand the work environment and what employees did and to develop the questions for the other methods of data gathering that would be used to analyze the current situation.

Telephone Interviews

Another method of quickly gathering information is telephone interviews. Many people believe that you cannot gather accurate and complete information through this method, but we have found it to be extremely workable in completing a Rapid Needs Analysis. Telephone interviews are conducted with as many key players as possible to gather background information that will be used to accurately identify the solution. Most often, the following people are involved in these interviews:

- a training and development management representative, who will have the education and training perspective and who will understand how this solution integrates with other performance improvement initiatives
- a senior management representative, who will be able to discuss the need from the point of view of the organization's strategic goals and speak to roles and accountabilities
- business unit representatives, who can speak to the specific business needs as related to the identified problem
- a human resource representative, who will be able to address how this need and its solution are linked to and will affect other human resource initiatives
- subject matter experts, who will be able to speak to the content, systems specifications, policies and procedures, and so forth.

Interviews are a highly recommended source of information, because participants can explore issues in more depth than through a survey or focus group. Additional questions can be asked to clarify meaning and ensure two-way communication. An added benefit of interviews is that they can be used to build rapport and support for the project.

Case Example: Telephone Interviews

The training group in the sales and marketing department of a major computer component manufacturing organization wanted to gather information from its reseller and distributor audience to aid in developing a new technical curriculum. The audience was geographically dispersed and had been "oversurveyed" in the previous six months. As an alternative to an online survey, electronic focus groups were held with a representative sample of the target audience. Additionally, telephone interviews were conducted with identified technical experts in the field. The interviews lasted 20 minutes and were conducted by the five employees in the training group. As a result, 60 interviews were conducted in fewer than three days. The quality of the information was good and was perceived as extremely helpful in understanding what technical skills were needed.

Determining the Methods to Use

Determining what method to use in collecting data to identify the current situation depends on the information you need, where it is located, who has it, and how much time it will take to tabulate the data collected. Table 2.1 can help you make this determination. The types and sources of information are listed in the left-hand and middle columns, and the most frequently used methods for gathering the information are listed in the right-hand column.

You can use worksheet 2.2 to document the methods you will use based on the information you need to gather. Transfer the information you need from the left-hand column of worksheet 2.1 to the left-hand column

Table 2.1: Determining the Data Collection Methods You Will Use

Type of Information	Source of Information	Most Frequently Used Methods
Organizational information	Strategic plans Mission statements Goals and objectives Organization charts Descriptions of major initiatives	Telephone or email contact with sponsor Telephone interview with management
Best practice information	Leaders in the industry Leaders in developing state-of-the-art performance solutions	Internet-based best practices literature search Telephone interviews
Past and current programs that address identified performance problem	Training	Telephone interview with training manager
	Processes	Telephone interview with managers Electronic focus group with managers or supervisors Online survey of target audience Job mapping
	Systems	Human resource information systems (HRIS) Other information systems
	Other initiatives	Electronic focus group with managers or supervisors Online survey of target audience
Audience information	Who How many Location	HRIS Contact with requester Interviews with managers or supervisors
	Education level Experience level	HRIS Electronic focus groups with managers, supervisors, and target audience Online survey of target audience
	Current job knowledge Current job skills Current job performance Physical conditions of the work area Nature and extent of supervision Others who influence or support the targeted audience	Electronic focus groups with managers, supervisors, and target audience Online survey of target audience Job mapping Observations

Table 2.1: Determining the Data Collection Methods You Will Use (continued)

Type of Information	Source of Information	Most Frequently Used Methods
Audience information	Current job attitudes	Electronic focus groups with managers, supervisors, and target audience Online survey of target audience Observations
	Position descriptions Performance plans	HRIS Contact with requester
Environmental issues	Constraints	Electronic focus groups with managers, supervisors, and target audience Online survey of target audience Job mapping Observations
	Politics Cultural factors	Telephone interviews with sponsors, managers, or supervisors Online survey of target audience Job mapping Observations
	Economic factors	Telephone interviews with sponsors, managers, or supervisors
Data to support performance problem and expected outcomes	Performance results	Electronic performance support system Other information systems Telephone interviews with sponsors, managers, and supervisors
	Customer feedback	Customer information system Other information systems Telephone interviews with sponsors, managers, and supervisors
	Lost revenue Increased costs	Other information systems Telephone interviews with sponsors, managers, and supervisors
	Attrition rates	HRIS Telephone interviews with sponsors, managers, and supervisors

of worksheet 2.2. In the right-hand column, identify the methods you will use to gather that information.

Developing the Instruments to Gather the Information

Now that you have determined the information you need and the methods you will use to gather the information, you can begin to develop the tools to gather the information. Table 2.2 lists some sample questions you should adapt for your purposes and the rationale associated with each question.

Examples of instruments for the most frequently used methods of data collection are provided in the sections that follow. Most of these instruments involve using technology, such as placing them on a Website or distributing them via email. The technical requirements and implementation are not addressed in this workbook.

Online Surveys

The development of online surveys, like the development of paper-based surveys, starts with the development of questions based on the information you need to collect (see table 2.2 for a listing of the information you need that you can gather through the use of an online survey). Question types 2, 3, 4, 5, and 6 listed in table 2.2 typically are used in surveys.

Most questions in a survey are closed response questions. *Closed response questions* list a fixed set of alternatives (much like a multiple-choice question), and the respondent is asked to choose the alternative that best identifies his or her choice, behavior, or opinion. An example of a closed survey question is

What is your highest level of education?
- ___ Grade school
- ___ High school
- ___ Some college
- ___ Trade school
- ___ College graduate (four-year)
- ___ Postgraduate degree

Open-ended questions have no fixed response categories and permit respondents to answer any way they wish. An example of an open-ended survey question is

What level of education have you attained?

_____

Worksheet 2.2 Methods Documentation Worksheet

Information Needed	Methods You Will Use
Organizational information	
Best practice information	
Past and current programs that address identified performance problem	
Audience information	
Environmental issues	
Data to support performance problem and expected outcomes	

Table 2.2: Developing Questions

Question Type	Sample Opening Questions	Purpose Behind Questions
1	Seek a general picture of the problem. • Is there a discrepancy? • Is there a problem? • What is going on in the problem? • What should be occurring? • Describe the situation as it is currently.	What are the problems? Who thinks there are problems? What should be going on? What is going on?
2	Seek details of the situation. • Describe the problem in detail. • Be specific in describing what is happening.	What should be happening? What is going on in detail? Who has the opinions? Where should attention be focused?
3	Seek proof of what incumbents know. • Can incumbents do what they say they can? • Do they know what they say they know? • Are they able to demonstrate performance?	What is the level of knowledge?
4	Seek feelings. • How do participants feel about the topic? • What are the feelings about the training or solution? • What is the perception of priorities? • What is the confidence level?	How do people feel about the problem? How do they feel about being trained or involved in another type of solution? What is the priority of this problem or training? Is there a belief that those trained could learn and demonstrate this knowledge or skill?
5	Seek causes. • What is creating the problem? • What is contributing to the problem? • How have they determined the cause?	What is the source of the problem? What or which of the causes are contributing to the problem?
6	Gather basic information about the participant. • Age? • Job type? • Sex? • Experience?	Who are the participants? Do demographics influence the responses?

Open-ended questions should be used sparingly, as they usually elicit a certain amount of irrelevant and repetitious information.

The sequence of the questions also is important. A poorly organized questionnaire can confuse respondents, bias their responses, and jeopardize the quality of the entire analysis effort. The sequence identified in table 2.3 has been used successfully in survey development.

Tool 2.1 is an example of an online survey. This survey was sent to customers of a technical training organization to determine the type of training needed in the future and how that training should be provided. This method was used in conjunction with electronic

Table 2.3: Successful Sequence of Questions in Paper or Email Surveys

Type of Question	Definition	Example
1. Introductory questions	Easy questions used to stimulate interest in continuing the survey without offending, threatening, or confusing	How long have you been an employee? What is your general level of satisfaction with the organization? ____Satisfied ____Neither satisfied nor dissatisfied ____Dissatisfied ____Highly dissatisfied
2. Sensitivity questions	Deal with sensitive topics such as controversial issues within your organization or personal questions that might be threatening. Sensitivity questions are better placed late in the survey; if respondents react negatively, they will abandon the survey.	What is the greatest challenge in your job today? How often do you receive coaching from your supervisor? How satisfied are you in your current job?
3. Related questions	Should be grouped together and possibly titled as such. For example, if you are designing a questionnaire to determine training needs, questions about management training should be grouped together and those about computer training should be grouped together.	Management training: What skills are important to the effectiveness of your job as a manager? ____Budgeting ____Planning ____Interviewing and hiring ____Performance management ____Coaching Computer training: What computer skills do you need to be effective in your job? ____Using word processing ____Developing presentations ____Using spreadsheets ____Using database reporting software

focus groups and telephone interviews with stake-holders. You will note that only nine questions were asked; the number of questions was limited to require less time to complete the survey and avoid respondent fatigue. This survey took respondents five to seven minutes to complete.

Electronic Focus Groups

Electronic focus groups use interview guides to ensure the consistency of responses across groups and to make sure that pertinent information is gathered.

The questions contained in the guides are similar to those of online surveys, and their development also is based on the information you need to collect (see table 2.1 for a listing of the information you need that you can gather through the use of electronic focus groups). Question types 1, 2, 3, 4, and 5 defined in table 2.2 typically are used in focus groups.

The questions asked in focus groups are similar to those used for surveys, but more open-ended questions are asked than in surveys to allow further probing as the groups are responding. The sequence of the

Table 2.3: Successful Sequence of Questions in Paper or Email Surveys (continued)

Type of Question	Definition	Example
4. Filter or screening questions	Establish the respondent's qualifications to answer subsequent questions. With a training needs survey, you may wish to screen respondents to determine if they are managers before asking them to answer questions about the need for management training.	What is your job title and job grade? (Write grade beside title.) ____Manager ____Supervisor ____Team lead ____Individual contributor ____Other_____
5. Reliability questions	Used when a question is important or controversial or the honesty or thoughtfulness of the respondent may be questioned. You can check the consistency of responses by asking virtually the same question in a somewhat different way and at a different place in the survey.	How likely are you to choose a sales position at the ABC Company? ____Very possible ____Somewhat possible ____Possible ____Not very likely ____Highly unlikely Then later in the survey: When you consider a sales position at the ABC Company, do you feel ____Excited ____Interested ____Indifferent ____Uncomfortable ____Frightened ____Other (Specify: _____)

questions should progress from general, nonthreatening topics to sensitivity and reliability questions (see table 2.3).

Tool 2.2 is an example of an interview guide for electronic focus groups. This guide was used to gather information from a group of call center managers at a funds management company to develop a new EPSS that would contain call-handling procedures and a process for dealing with irate callers and escalating calls. The focus group was completed in one hour.

Best Practices Literature Search

Best practices literature searches involve researching how other organizations have solved their performance problems and can help you identify industry trends. Identifying competitors and gathering information related to their practices is frequently informative. In addition, some companies find great value in looking beyond their own industry to learn what best practices are driving WLP in other, noncompeting companies.

The Internet probably is the most effective way to gather this information and is the major tool for this type of information gathering. However, before beginning your search it is important to organize your thoughts about what you want to discover about the topics and companies you have chosen to research.

Table 2.4 can be used to organize your best practice search by identifying key phrases to use with search engines and sites. In column 1, the most typical

Tool 2.1: Online Survey Example

Position: _____ **Location:** _____

Number of Years with Current Employer: _____ **Number of Years in Profession:** _____

1. In the past six months I have been involved in the following training programs:
   (Programs listed here to be checked yes or no)

                                                                Yes   **No**

   _____ ☐   ☐

   _____ ☐   ☐

2. I would benefit in the future from training in
   (Programs listed here and preferences indicated using the rating scale from Strongly agree to Strongly disagree)

	Strongly agree	Agree	Somewhat agree	Somewhat disagree	Disagree	Strongly disagree
_____	____	____	____	____	____	____
_____	____	____	____	____	____	____
_____	____	____	____	____	____	____

3. What training do you need in the future that is not listed in question 2? _____

4. Technical training programs would be more effective and efficient for me if they were delivered

	Strongly agree	Agree	Somewhat agree	Somewhat disagree	Disagree	Strongly disagree
In person	____	____	____	____	____	____
By conference call	____	____	____	____	____	____
By CD-ROM	____	____	____	____	____	____
By satellite	____	____	____	____	____	____
By e-learning	____	____	____	____	____	____
Combination of methods	____	____	____	____	____	____
Other methods:_____						

5. The depth of technical information in the training programs has met my needs in the past.

        ____   ____   ____   ____   ____   ____

6. The training programs are offered when I need them.

        ____   ____   ____   ____   ____   ____

7. It is easy for me to participate in the training programs.

        ____   ____   ____   ____   ____   ____

8. The training programs help me be more effective in my business or job.

        ____   ____   ____   ____   ____   ____

9. What comments do you have about our training programs?

_____

Tool 2.2: Electronic Focus Group Interview Guide Example

Introductory comments:

- purpose of focus group
- participants' role
- expected results
- ground rules (including the use of technology)
- confidentiality of responses
- ask for comments and questions.

1. Describe the purpose of the call center. Why does it exist; what function does it serve?

2. Describe the call center environment.

3. Describe your role in the call center.

4. Currently, what procedures do employees follow to handle customer calls?

5. Are employees handling calls as you expect them to? Why or why not?

6. Specifically, are they following the procedures that are in the manuals?

7. If no, why not? What barriers exist that prevent them from following the procedures?

8. Do they follow the processes in place for handling irate customers?

9. If no, why not? What barriers exist that prevent them from following the processes?

10. Do they escalate calls as required? Why or why not?

(continued next page)

Tool 2.2: Electronic Focus Group Interview Guide Example (continued)

11. If no, why not? What barriers exist that prevent them from escalating calls as required?

12. Please describe an average day in the life of a call center rep. What is he or she expected to do, when, and under what conditions?

13. How do you think the electronic performance support system (EPSS) will change that?

14. What information do think needs to be included in the EPSS, and why?

15. In your opinion, what will be the most difficult part of implementing the EPSS? Why?

16. What type of training or information should call center employees have to prepare them to fully utilize the EPSS?

17. What role should supervisors and managers have in designing the EPSS? What role should employees have?

18. What else do you have to say about the call center, the call center reps, their call handling performance, and their tools?

---

information researched in a best practice study is listed. In column 2, corresponding key phrases to use in the search are listed. Finally, in column 3, the types of Websites to search are listed.

The following are among the Web search engines that can be used to find sites with useful information:

- www.google.com
- www.search.com
- www.ussc.alltheweb.com
- www.altavista.com
- www.yahoo.com
- www.go.com
- www.excite.com
- www.lycos.com
- www.webcrawler.com.

There also are several Web browsers (software applications that access sites across the World Wide Web). The most commonly used are Spry Mosaic, Netscape Navigator, and Microsoft Internet Explorer. A listing of frequently used WLP Websites is provided in table 2.5.

Job Mapping

Job mapping involves discovering and recording the details of the tasks involved in doing a job so that

Table 2.4: Organizing Internet Best Practices Research

Topic to Be Researched	Key Phrases to Use	Types of Sites to Search
Competitor practices (your industry's competitors)	Competitor name Competitor name and topic of research Industry and topic of research	Competitors' own sites Industry periodical sites
Professional practices (practices specific to a profession, like training, engineering, and sales)	Professional practice Professional practice and topic of research Industry and professional practice	Professional practice newsgroups E-publications Discussion lists Professional publications and journals
Industry standards	Topic of research Topic of research and industry Type of standard	Professional practice newsgroups E-publications Discussion lists Quality organizations and periodicals
New trends (specific to the type of business problem or performance gap)	Topic of research Topic of research and industry Topic of research and profession	Professional practice newsgroups E-publications Discussion lists Paper publications and journals Professional publications and journals
Outside industry practices (best practices among those who have similar jobs but are not in same industry)	Type of practice and topic of research	Newsgroups E-publications Discussion lists Paper publications and journals Professional publications and journals

you can identify the knowledge, skills, expected performance, and barriers to doing the job. The Job Mapping Worksheet (table 2.6) not only provides a method of documentation but will prompt you to review all aspects of the job while gathering information from employees. The categories you want to map with the audience are listed in the left-hand column, and the specific information you should gather for that component is listed in the right-hand column.

Observations

The Observation Worksheet (tool 2.3) is used to document data gathered in an unstructured observation—for example, while observing workers to see

what their jobs entail on a day-to-day basis, or while seeking to identify differences between two jobs that are supposedly the same but are performed in different locations. You can also use this type of worksheet to capture information about the environment and its barriers or to validate information collected through other data collection methods. This worksheet can be used to document observations with individual employees or the environment in general.

Telephone Interviews

An interview guide is as important in getting the information desired from telephone interviews as it is in conducting online focus groups. In fact, the ques-

Table 2.5: WLP Websites

Website	Web Address
AskEric	http://ericir.syr.edu
Adult Education Collection at Syracuse University	http://wwwweb.syr.edu/~ancharte/resource.html
Big Dog's HR Development Page	http://wwwnwlink.com/~donclark/hrd.html
CMC Information Services	http://www.december.com/cmc/info
Training Net	http://www.trainingnet.com
World Economic & Business Development	http://www.mecnet.org/edr
Home for Internet Planners	http://www.Kensho.com/hip
Consultant Resource Center	http://www.consultant-center.com
Computer Training Network	http://www.crctraining.com/training
HR Headquarters	http://www.hrhq.com
Internet Training Center Training Links	http://www.std.com/~walthowe/trnglinks.html
San Diego State University Ed Web	http://www.edweb.sdsu.edu
Training Forum Speakers Database	http://www.trainingforum.com
Training Resource Access Center	http://trainingaccesscenter.com
Educom	http://educom.edu
National Center for Vocational Research	http://www.ncver.edu.au/ncver.htm

Table 2.6: Job Mapping Process Components

Mapping Components	Information to Be Gathered
Job	Identify the job that will be mapped and diagram how that job supports the organizational goals or efforts. Identify the business drivers that affect the job.
Tasks	List the tasks performed for the job being mapped.
Conditions	Identify the characteristics of the workplace, such as equipment, noise level, interruptions, and location. Identify any conditions that may be barriers to getting tasks completed (e.g., lack of resources).
Standards	Identify any standards that can be used to measure the task quality, quantity, or timeliness.
Knowledge requirements	Identify any necessary knowledge requirements for systems, procedures, regulations, safety, and so forth.
Skill requirements	Identify any necessary skill requirements for systems, procedures, regulations, safety, and so forth.

Tool 2.3: Observation Worksheet Example

Job type observed:

Observation site:

Environment or people observed:

Date of observation: _____

Time started: _____

Time ended: _____

1. Reasons for this observation (check all that apply):

    _____Seeking details of optimal job performance

    _____Seeking details of actual job performance

    _____Observing for barriers, potential success factors, or problems that occur

    _____Observing for general information

2. Describe identified performance need (be as detailed and specific as possible):

3. Identify business drivers to which this job contributes:

4. Note observations in five- to 10-minute increments:

General Observations: Behaviors, Skills, or Knowledge Demonstrated	Comments and Details

tions frequently are the same and are similarly developed. Question types 1, 2, 3, 4, 5, and 6 defined in table 2.2 typically are used in telephone interview guides.

Tool 2.4 is an example of an interview guide for a telephone interview. This guide was used in interviews with product managers who were considered technical experts in the subject matter in which resellers and distributors were to be trained. Each interview took 20 minutes to complete.

Testing the Data Gathering Instruments

An important part of step 2 of the Rapid Needs Analysis process is testing the instruments you will use to gather the data on the current situation before using them with the entire audience or audience sample. No matter how experienced you are in developing these types of tools, it still is sound practice to test them on a small sample of the target audience. Although testing may seem like a time-consuming activity, skipping it could result in re-work or undermine the credibility of the analysis project. Testing instruments for online surveys, electronic focus groups, observations, and telephone interviews is addressed in the next section.

Gathering the Information

The next activity in step 2 of the Rapid Needs Analysis process is to quickly gather the information you need using the methods you identified. How to jump-start the information gathering is detailed for each method.

Tool 2.4: Telephone Interview Guide Example

1. To clarify, what is your position, and how long have you been in it?

2. What products do you manage?

3. In general, what technical knowledge and skills would a reseller need to sell and support each of these products?

4. In general, what technical knowledge and skills would a distributor need to distribute each of these products?

To drill down a bit further:

5. What specific knowledge and skills would a reseller need to be proficient in selling and supporting these products? Please be specific for each product.

6. What specific knowledge and skills would a distributor need to be proficient in distributing these products? Please be specific for each product.

7. If there were no limits at all placed on what training could be offered to resellers, what would you offer?

8. What training would you offer to distributors?

9. What training is absolutely essential for resellers? for distributors?

10. Is there anything else you would like to say about the technical training needs of resellers and distributors?

Online Surveys

The following guidelines will assist you in implementing an online survey:

1. *Identify and contact the population to be surveyed.* Once you have identified the population you want to survey, you should consider sending an email explaining the purpose of and need for the survey to alert respondents to what is expected of them and why. Clear communication about the "why" usually will increase the quality of responses and the response rate.

2. *Follow proper sample selection procedures.* To determine the sampling frame, you must first have a list of the entire population. In organizations you can get this information from the HRIS. The next step is choosing the respondents from the list who will form your sampling frame. Simple and systematic random sampling are the most effective methods of sampling to use in Rapid Needs Analysis, as they are the least complicated and will take less time and fewer resources.

    In simple random sampling, each name is given a number, and numbers are chosen randomly. There are computer programs that can do a simple random sample. Systematic random sampling, usually done with larger populations, adapts the process above by choosing, for example, one name from every 2,500.

3. *Design the survey instrument.* A sample of a survey instrument is provided in tool 2.1.

4. *Pretest the survey.* You should review your survey with others in your department, the managers of the audience to be surveyed, or a few members of the audience before distributing it to your sample. Ask your reviewers whether the questions are clear and whether the survey is comprehensive and relevant for the audience.

5. *Distribute the survey.* The last step in implementing online surveys is to distribute the survey electronically using the technology and technical expertise available within your organization.

Electronic Focus Groups

Planning is essential for conducting a quality focus group. A carefully constructed and communicated agenda is necessary, and participants should be thoroughly briefed about the purpose of the focus group and their role before attending the focus group session.

The client should review the questions or script before you conduct the focus groups. You may also want to test your script with a segment of the focus group audience before holding the real sessions.

The following guidelines will help you organize and implement an electronic focus group:

1. *Determine who should participate in the focus group.* Focus groups usually are made up of six to 12 people and last between 1.5 and two hours. The participants in these groups usually have similar job characteristics. For example, all participants might be managers in the sales department, or they all might be employees who have been with the company fewer than three years and have attended the Basic Communications course. Focus groups should only rarely contain employees with any type of reporting relationship.

2. *Determine the information needed and write the interview guide.* An example of an interview guide for a focus group is provided in tool 2.2.

3. *Pretest the interview guide.* You should review the interview guide with others in your department, the managers of the audience to be interviewed, or a few members of the audience before you facilitate the group. Pretesting is critical in ensuring that the questions make sense and are in the right order.

4. *Notify the participants.* Before launching the electronic focus group, notify participants by email to request their participation and inform them of the purpose of the group, the desired outcome, and how the information from the group will be used. Be sure to clarify what the participant's role is in the focus group.

5. *Launch the group.* The last step in implementing focus groups is to facilitate them electronically using the technology and technical expertise available within your organization. Specifically, you should be sure to

   - collect demographic information

   - review the purpose of the focus group

   - ask the questions

   - close the session

   - ensure that follow-up occurs with participants; let them know the results of the focus group as deemed appropriate by your customers and management.

Best Practices Literature Searches

The following guidelines can help you jump-start a best practices literature search:

1. *Determine all key words that define the project.* A few of the many possibilities are *quality, TQM, Deming,* and *team management.*

2. *Identify all companies that are successful at the type of solution identified, considered to be competition, or have best practices.* Best practice companies are those recognized by peers or WLP professional associations for their innovative or quality practices as measured against a set of standards. Baldridge award criteria are an example of standards used to identify "the cream of the crop."

3. *Complete an industry search in either your industry or an industry that is known to be successful in this type of solution or both.*

4. *Complete a search by type of periodical or service (e.g., all issues of* Harvard Business Review) *for like topics.*

5. *Conduct a search using the business drivers as search words.*

Table 2.5 lists workplace learning and performance Websites that can assist you in implementing this type of research.

Job Mapping

You can use the following guidelines to implement a job mapping session:

1. *Identify the audience members and prepare them for the session.* A sample of the target audience typically is selected for job mapping. Sometimes a mix of low, medium, and high performers are included in these sessions so that you have a good cross-section of employees represented. These groups always comprise employees in the same type of job.

   To make use of available time, it is helpful to ask those attending the session to track their time for a day or two before the meeting and to be prepared to discuss how they do their jobs. Valuable time can be wasted if attendees do not know the purpose of the meeting or are not properly prepared. It is also important to stress that the information gathered will not be attributed to individual employees.

2. *Determine the information you need.* The information you should gather during a job mapping session includes

   - specific job tasks
   - characteristics of the workplace, such as equipment used, noise level, interruptions, and workplace characteristics
   - barriers to completing the tasks
   - standards that can be used to measure task quality, quantity, or timeliness
   - knowledge and skill requirements for systems, procedures, regulations, safety, and so forth.

3. *Develop the mapping sequence and documentation form.* Job mapping usually is facilitated following the order of steps in a process (if it exists) or activities that happen throughout the day. Once you have identified the information that is critical to collect, you can determine the sequence of the session. Table 2.6 can help you document the job mapping process.

4. *Conducting the session.* Most job mapping sessions take at least three hours to get to the detail needed to thoroughly understand the job. Expert facilitation is essential so that the walk-through and resulting discussion do not get bogged down in irrelevant details. It is important to remember that this is not a problem-solving or decision-making session.

The first step in job mapping is to break down the job content into easily understandable individual segments and then gather information on each segment. These job segments include the specific activities performed, the responsibilities and accountabilities of the employees performing them, and the expected results and the mission or outcome of the activities performed.

The next step is to collect data on the skills, abilities, knowledge, and education required for the job. This data should be compared to an existing description of the job. Data regarding the context of the job within the organization and its position and relationship to other positions should be collected, as well as performance standards and selection criteria that may be used for the job.

The environment in which the job is performed and where it is physically located are also important to the job analysis. Environmental factors include the physical conditions of the work area, the physical location, and the nature and extent of supervision.

Observation

The following guidelines can be used to conduct an observation:

1. *Schedule the observation.* It is best to schedule observations at random times so that you can review performance or the environment in general under different conditions (e.g., busy time of month, slow time, in a customer problem situation, when a system is down). If this is not possible due to time constraints, as is often the case in Rapid Needs Analysis, then make sure you have observed several different employees doing the same job.

   You should inform employees when they will be observed, by whom, and for what purpose. Clear communication about what you are doing, with whom, and why is necessary to prevent unnecessary anxiety about your presence.

2. *Develop an observation worksheet.* Tool 2.3 is a sample of this type of worksheet.

3. *Introduce the Observation Worksheet (tool 2.3) and conduct the observation.* If you are conducting an observation of an individual employee, be sure to show the employee the Observation Worksheet, and then position yourself to conduct the observation in a place that will not interfere with the employee's work. Most observations take about 30 to 45 minutes to complete.

Telephone Interviews

You can use the following guidelines to conduct a quality telephone interview:

1. *Determine who needs to be interviewed.* Candidates typically include members of management, subject matter experts, key stakeholders, and others who have critical information regarding the effectiveness, intent, content, or competency levels of the identified solution.

2. *Determine the information you need from the interview, and write the questions accordingly.* Tool 2.4 is a sample of a telephone interview guide.

3. *Remember to include demographic information.* You can use it to trace any trends based on background, experience, or education.

4. *Develop an interview guide that can serve as an agenda.* This guide will help you achieve your purpose, establish a relationship, track your progress during the interview, and complete the interview in the allotted time.

5. *Review the questions with a sample group of people who will be interviewed or test the questions with a sample set of interviewees.* A review is critical in working out the kinks in the questions and ensuring you will gather the information you need.

6. *Set up the interviews.* This can be done most effectively via email. Be clear about why you are conducting the interviews, the time it will take, and the desired outcome. Also explain how the information from the interviews will be used. Once the interview is confirmed, send the questions to the person to be interviewed and ask him or her to review them before the interview. This will save time and yield higher quality information.

7. *Conduct the interview.* It is important to do the following things at the beginning of the interview: introduce yourself, discuss the goals of the interview, introduce the project and provide background information as appropriate, and emphasize that all responses will be confidential.

Identifying Gaps and Errors in the Information Collected

When you have gathered all of the information you need to identify the current situation, it is time to determine if there are any gaps or errors in the information. Have you collected all the information you need? Is it accurate? This checkpoint is critical because the data you have gathered will be used to determine the gap between expected performance and current performance and to begin to develop the requirements for the identifying the solution.

Worksheet 2.3 can assist you in completing this activity and help you identify any additional information that you may need. In the far left-hand column, enter the information you need that you have already noted in worksheet 2.1. Then, in the next column, note the information you have gathered. In the third column, indicate whether the information you gathered is adequate and accurate, and if not, identify what else is needed in the far right-hand column. If you think it is necessary (and politically wise), you might want to review this information with the project requester or sponsor.

Collecting Additional Information If Needed

If you determine that you need to collect additional information, you should plan for what you need and how you will collect it. Typically this will include going back to a provider of the information to validate the data or back to the environment to gather information from other members of the audience or their managers.

One thing to keep in mind when collecting additional information is the risk involved in taking more time from the information sources; the time of sponsors, requesters, the target audience, and managers of the target audience is valuable. Offending those you need information from may be a greater threat to the project's success than not having all the information with total accuracy. In addition, with the time constraints of Rapid Needs Analysis, the risk of taking too long to get all the data may outweigh the risk of having some degree of incomplete or inaccurate data.

Worksheet 2.4 can help you plan how you will collect the additional information needed to make sure your data is complete and accurate. In the left-hand column, transfer the additional information needed, identified in the left-hand column in worksheet 2.3. In the middle column, note how you will collect this information and from whom. In the right-hand column, identify the risk to the project in going back for more information or validating existing information.

Worksheet 2.3: Identifying Gaps and Errors

Information Needed	Information Gathered	Information Adequate and Accurate? (yes or no)	If No, What Else Is Needed?
Organizational information: Goals and objectives Mission statements Other major initiatives	Business plan Strategic plan Data from interview with senior management Data from focus group with department managers	Yes and no. Have gathered enough information but there seems to be a discrepancy among senior managers regarding the goals and objectives.	Will need to clarify discrepancy—will call project sponsor.

Worksheet 2.4: Planning Worksheet for Collecting Additional Information

Additional Information Needed	How You Will Collect It and From Whom	Risk in Collecting It
Need to clarify the discrepancy among senior managers regarding the goals and objectives.	By email with project sponsor.	Low risk—this clarification is essential in getting to the right solution.

Chapter Summary

In this chapter, the second step of the Rapid Needs Analysis process was introduced and discussed. Case examples were presented throughout the chapter that illustrate how several different organizations collected the information needed to identify the current situation. Determining where to get this information and what methods to use were addressed, and examples of data collection instruments were provided. Guidelines for gathering the information, as well as identifying gaps and inaccuracies in the data, were presented for each data collection method. Finally, how to determine if you should collect more information based on the risks to the project was addressed.

Discussion Questions

The following questions are provided to help you apply what you learned in this chapter:

- From whom or what system will you gather the information you need to gather?

- What methods of information gathering will you use, and why?

- Who will you contact to assist with the technical requirements of gathering data electronically?

   _____

   _____

- What data gathering instruments will you have to develop, and who in your organization can help you develop them?

   _____

   _____

- Who will do the actual data gathering?

   _____

   _____

- Is it possible to anticipate where you may have information gaps or inaccuracies?

   _____

   _____

- How will you know if it is worth the risk to gather more information if it is needed?

   _____

   _____

3

Step 3: Analyzing the Data

Step 3 of the Rapid Needs Analysis process involves analyzing the data you collected during step 2, identifying the current situation. Once you understand what the data means, you will be ready to compare the current situation to the expected outcomes and then to identify performance gaps. You will then be able to recommend a solution or solutions that will close the gap as quickly and effectively as possible.

Countless texts and manuals have been written about how to analyze data. For the purposes of Rapid Needs Analysis and this workbook, it is not our goal to educate you in all aspects of data analysis, but rather to provide you with a fast and sound approach to analyzing data so that it can be used to identify workplace learning and performance solutions.

In our experience, WLP practitioners frequently get stuck in this step of rapid analysis. There seems to be some deep mystery (and misunderstanding) of data analysis that makes it seem harder than it is. The mere mention of data analysis sends some people running, others into a panic, and still others to outside resources that may or may not be needed.

The main consideration in analyzing the data collected in the previous step is to quickly identify the results so that you are able to make decisions regarding what the solution should be and how it will be developed. This chapter provides information to help you do this.

At the end of step 3 you will know

- the current situation and how it relates to the business drivers, business needs, and performance needs that were identified in step 1

- the gap between current performance and expected performance

- how to link the performance gap to potential solutions

- the performance solution that is the "best" for closing the performance gap

- the performance measures for the solution.

Case Examples

Case examples are provided later in this chapter for each of the three types of data analysis used in Rapid Needs Analysis.

Step 3 Activities

You will complete the following 10 activities in this step of the Rapid Needs Analysis process:

1. planning the data analysis
2. choosing the type of analysis
3. identifying data bias
4. analyzing the data
5. interpreting the results
6. aligning results with business drivers and business needs
7. identifying the performance gap
8. evaluating the identified solution
9. identifying performance measures linked to expected outcomes
10. validating the identified solution with the requester, sponsor, and stakeholders.

This chapter explains each activity in detail and provides the tools you need to complete this step.

Planning the Data Analysis

Planning ahead for the data analysis will save time and help you identify the resources needed up front.

Table 3.1 can help you plan for analyzing the data collected in the previous step of the Rapid Needs Analysis process. All activities that you need to complete for data analysis are identified, along with the purpose of each activity and the time required to complete each one.

Choosing the Type of Analysis

The next activity in analyzing the data is choosing the type of analysis you will use. The three most common types used in Rapid Needs Analysis are content analysis, process analysis, and quantitative analysis.

The type of analysis you should use is dependent on the type of data you have and the purpose for which you will be using it. It's important that the data tells the story it needs to tell so you arrive at the correct conclusions and recommendations. For example, you would not be able to use content analysis to determine the average length of phone calls coming into a call center, because this would require analysis of statistics (quantitative analysis). Nor would you use it to analyze the flow of work when you need to identify a process (process analysis). You would, however, be able to use content analysis to determine the type of call coming in and the types of questions asked, which are both related to content.

Each of the three types of data analysis is described below and a case example given of how each was used. Table 3.2 can help you determine the type of data analysis to use for the data gathering methods that were introduced in chapter 2.

Content Analysis

Content analysis is a method of analyzing qualitative data in a systematic, objective, and quantitative manner. It involves the analysis and classification of data into major content areas. This method involves five steps:

1. identifying the strategic focus, business purpose, and objectives

Table 3.1: Data Analysis Planning

Data Analysis Activity	Purpose of Activity	Time Required
Planning the data analysis	To identify the resources needed for the data analysis	0.2–0.5 day
Choosing the type of analysis	To choose the method of data analysis linked to the method of data collection to ensure that the analysis is accurate	0.2–0.5 day
Identifying data bias	To identify biases that could prejudice or corrupt the data	0.2–0.5 day
Analyzing the data	To analyze the data and quantify results	0.3–1.0 day
Interpreting the results	To make sense of the results of the data analysis	0.3–1.0 day
Aligning results with business drivers and business needs	To make sure the results will lead to a solution that will increase performance and meet the identified business need	0.2–0.5 day
Identifying the performance gap	To identify the difference between the expected or required performance and the current performance	0.2–0.5 day
Evaluating the identified solution	To ensure that the solution you recommend will be successful in providing the desired results	0.2–0.5 day
Identifying performance measures linked to expected outcomes	To identify measures that will be used to evaluate the solution's success	0.2–0.5 day
Validating the identified solution with the requester, sponsor, and stakeholders	To make certain the requester, sponsor, and stakeholders agree that the identified solution is the right one	0.2–0.5 day

Table 3.2: Linking the Data Gathering Method to Type of Data Analysis

Data Gathering Method	Type of Data Analysis	Rationale
Online surveys	Quantitative analysis	Most survey responses are statistical, or closed, data. When conducted online, surveys can be quickly sorted and tabulated by downloading the data into a data analysis program such as Access or Excel.
	Content analysis	Content analysis is used to analyze the responses to open-ended questions either electronically, through key word searches, or manually. Electronic and manual content analysis takes about the same amount of time.
Electronic focus groups	Content analysis	The data from focus groups is qualitative and requires sorting data into major content areas.
Best practices literature search	Content analysis	The data resulting from a best practices literature search also is qualitative and therefore requires sorting data into major content areas.
Job mapping	Process analysis	The data resulting from job mapping identifies the components or steps of a work process and details the tasks involved in doing specific jobs. The tools, resources, and methods used to do a job should also be detailed in this type of analysis.
Observations	Process analysis	As in job mapping, data from observations should reveal a job process, job tasks, and tools.
Telephone interviews	Content analysis	Most telephone interview responses are responses to open-ended questions and thus highly qualitative.
	Quantitative analysis	Many interview responses to questions are statistical (closed data), such as demographic information (e.g., number of years in job, number of years in school).

2. organizing the findings by the business purpose and objectives

3. classifying the findings by categories or subcategories under the purpose and objectives

4. determining the range, variations, consistencies, and inconsistencies of the data

5. validating the key findings and recommendations.

If you are using the data to identify knowledge and skill transfer and a new solution needs to be developed, you should use content analysis. Content analysis most typically is used to analyze focus group data, interview data, and the comment sections of surveys.

Case Example: Content Analysis

The purpose of the analysis was to assess a large and diverse population of supervisors to determine the key training needs for a new supervisory program. Electronic focus groups were one of four methods used in developing the supervisory training curriculum. The focus groups were used with supervisors in the key geographic locations of the company to ascertain their thoughts about current training and determine their perceptions regarding their own needs individually and as a group. Three separate groups were conducted.

Content analysis was used to present the data in a systematic, objective, and quantitative manner. The data was presented in major content areas, which was ideal for identifying the supervisors' individual thoughts about key curriculum categories. See tool 3.1 for a sample of data collected and its presentation following analysis.

Process Analysis

Most commonly, process analysis is used in analyzing the results of data collection using observation or job mapping. Process analysis identifies the components or steps of a work process. Tools, resources, and methods that accompany each step are detailed. Often worksheets (e.g., see table 2.6) are used to record the process being analyzed, and problems and oppor-

tunities within the specific performance context are noted, as is anecdotal information. Process analysis combined with a form of quantitative analysis can be a very powerful tool for determining data trends, validating findings, and making strong recommendations.

Case Example: Process Analysis

The purpose of the analysis project was to identify competencies for employees of a call center. Observation was one of the methods used to gain an understanding of the environment in which the employees worked and the consequent impact of this environment on skills and behaviors. Process analysis was used to determine environmental factors for the competencies. See tool 3.2 for a sample of data collected and its presentation following analysis.

Quantitative Analysis

In quantitative analysis, data is analyzed statistically. Most often a computer is used to support the compilation and display of quantitative analysis. Data is then abstracted from the analysis and communicated or presented appropriately. If your method of data

---

Tool 3.1: Sample of Case Study Content Analysis

Sample of the Data Captured

Question 5. What are your biggest challenges, and what training is needed to prepare for these challenges?

Biggest challenges:
- lack of direction
- poor morale
- displaced workers training staff who will replace them
- directives to lower costs and close operating plants
- unfair bonus system
- negative attitudes
- need to cope with change
- management of the quality and quantity of information about change
- need to be proactive
- requirement to do more with less, less with less, and different things with less and orienting customers to resulting changes.

Training needs:
- improvement in staff morale and motivation
- enhancement of communication skills
- communication training in working with a national and international company
- support of the company with minimal information
- handling the fear, anger, and distrust of employees coming from companies acquired by the company.

Tool 3.1: Sample of Case Study Content Analysis (continued)

Question 6. What skills or knowledge do you need to manage your team and "to do more with less"?

- Computer skills
- Methods for working faster
- Team training
- Help in learning ways to do things differently
- Direction on what has to be done (priorities are not clear)
- More leadership from upper management
- Compensation and recognition
- Teamwork, empowerment, and employee-management relationships
- Information about how to empower employees to be competent—making it OK for staff so they don't have to fear being punished by peers for their competence
- Communicating change, strategy, organization needs, and direction
- Managing, hiring, and supervising temporary workers
- Managing union relations; union relations are out of their hands
- Tools and skills to support the high degree of employee accountability for skill development; employees ultimately must take responsibility for developing their own performance
- Budget management from a financial analysis viewpoint
- Cost-benefit analysis
- Assisting employees in setting financial priorities.

Presentation of the Data Following Analysis

The key findings from the focus groups led to the following recommendations:

1. An initial orientation to the supervisory position is needed.

2. The managers of the supervisors need to be more involved in the overall supervisory development process.

3. The current supervisory curriculum needs enhancement to include the following topics:
   - change management
   - dealing with poor morale
   - how to motivate employees
   - communication
   - handling employee fear, anger, and distrust.

4. The following modules or sections should also be added to the supervisory curriculum:
   - compensation and recognition
   - teamwork, empowerment, and employee-management relationships
   - communicating change, strategy, organization needs, direction
   - hiring practices, promotions, and job design
   - employee performance
   - union relations and temporary workers
   - workforce and skill development
   - workforce diversity
   - financial strength and conducting business practices effectively and with high quality.

5. The supervisory curriculum needs to include content that addresses how to use technology to work faster and more easily.

6. The supervisory curriculum should be required for all supervisors within the organization and should be linked to core supervisory competencies.

Tool 3.2: Sample of Case Study Process Analysis

Sample of the Data Captured

Call Center Service Support Observation Sheet

Type of call: How-to question

Customer concern, problem, or question:
- can't get application to print chart
- screen blank after entering data in address field on screen 7
- wants application to interface with database reporting software.

Result or outcome (e.g., resolved, escalated, call back):
- resolved within one minute—problem solving
- escalated to Team Lead (bug in software that was previously untracked)
- call back (research done with Tec [technical expert]).

Source of workflow: Telephone

Process used:
- identifies self
- asks for customer ID number
- asks for problem ID number
- enters both in computer
- calls up problem worksheet
- asks for problem description
- enters problem description in computer
- uses problem tracking and resolution system to review if problem is common or for more information.

Communication vehicles used: email, voicemail

Follow-up required: Primarily used tools and Tec for follow-up. One call required Team Lead.

Tools used in process and comments:
- problem tracking and resolution software, email, voicemail
- average time spent:
  —with customer or online: 40 minutes per hour
  —researching: 10 minutes every fifth call
  —responding and follow-up: one in six calls.

Sample of Presentation of the Data Following Analysis

Observations were used to determine what was going on in the work environment. The findings included the following:

1. Environmental factors included high noise level, constant interruption while on phone by other members, no indication of type of call or caller mood, and not necessarily having recent product information or the same updates that customer had obtained through sales representatives.

2. The following types of calls were received: 32% problem resolution, 22% how-to or help questions (which could be answered by available online help), 15% complaint, 13% questions unrelated to product or support (e.g., location of company, employment opportunities), 11% sales-related questions, and 7% follow-up calls.

3. The most prevalent workplace communication vehicles were staff meetings, bulletin boards, email, and voice mail. Email was the most commonly used.

4. Work climate factors included such things as Team Lead motivation, other member morale, teamwork, and willingness to share information or workloads.

5. The flow of work was driven by the telephone, email, and team supervisor. Most workflow was completed in a reactive format; however, some was project driven.

collection results in statistical data such as that derived from a customer feedback survey, then you would use quantitative analysis.

Case Example: Quantitative Analysis

The purpose of this analysis was to identify best practice companies for information management performance solutions. One of the methods used was an electronic survey of 400 managers of WLP in *Fortune 500* companies.

The survey data was analyzed using quantitative analysis. In this case SPSS-pc, a statistical software package, was used to generate simple frequencies, percentages, and cross tabulations. Text comments were analyzed by grouping based on content and sorting using Microsoft Excel. Tool 3.3 gives a sample of data collected and its presentation following analysis. The sample of data is from the actual computer results.

Identifying Data Bias

Data bias refers to ways in which the data might be prejudiced or corrupted and can lead to flawed data analysis. It is extremely important to identify data bias during qualitative analysis such as content and process analysis. If data bias is not discovered and dealt with, your solution will most probably end up being off the mark because the information used to recommend it was incorrect.

Although bias almost always exists, acknowledging it can help you avoid misinterpreting the data. One potential source of bias is strong beliefs about the topic being researched on the part of the person analyzing the data. For example, let's say the analyst is a designer who has a strong belief that a certain solution is the only one that should be used. This person has always designed classroom training and has resisted other delivery methods in the past. These beliefs could influence the way the analyst conducts the analysis if, for example, he or she emphasizes data that favors classroom training.

Another way that data can be contaminated is through preconceived ideas about the topic being analyzed. For example, the senior manager of the target audience has made it clear that he or she will support the performance solution only if it focuses on technical procedures. The manager does not want employees to have "soft skills" training, even if it is important to achieving success on the job. The strong opinions of important decision makers can influence how the data is analyzed and results interpreted.

Tool 3.3: Sample of Case Study Quantitative Analysis

Sample of the Data Captured

Total number of responses: 179 from 400 possibilities (45% return rate)

For questions 1 through 4, an average number cannot be computed because the list of valid responses is composed of ranges.

Demographics

Question 1. How long have you been involved in training and development? (178 responses)

Number of Years	Number of Responses	%
< 1	8	4.5
1–2	24	13.5
3–5	38	21.3
6–10	34	19.1
11–20	59	33.1
> 20	15	8.4

(continued on next page)

Tool 3.3: Sample of Case Study Quantitative Analysis (continued)

Question 2. Are you an in-house trainer, external provider, or other? (179 responses)

Type of Trainer	Number of Responses	%
In-house trainer	96	53.6
External provider	38	21.2
Other	45 (including managerial positions)	25.1

Question 3. How many employees are served by your training department? (146 responses, excluding "does not apply" [32 responses] and "does not have a training department" [1 response])

Number of Employees	Number of Responses	%
< 250	32	21.9
250–499	22	15.1
500–999	23	15.8
1,000–1,999	22	15.1
> 2,000	47	32.2

Question 4. What is the size of the training staff in your business unit? (173 responses, excluding "not applicable" [6 responses])

Staff Size	Number of Responses	%
1	28	16.2
2–5	65	37.6
6–10	26	15.0
11–20	15	8.7
21–50	19	11.0
> 50	20	11.6

Question 5. What percentage of training does your organization provide using internal staff (versus external providers)?

Year	Percentage	Number of Valid Answers
1997	70.6	143
2000	61.0	138

Question 6a. To what extent do you agree that companies will use intranet or Internet technology as their primary tool for delivering training? (Averages were computed using the following values: 1 = strongly disagree, 2 = disagree, 3 = neutral, 4 = agree, 5 = strongly agree.)

Year	Average Response Score
1997	2.2
2000	3.6

Tool 3.3: Sample of Case Study Quantitative Analysis (continued)

Sample of Presentation of the Data Following Analysis

1. *Length of time involved in training and development.* The most frequent work experience for survey respondents was 10–20 years, followed by 2–5 years. Overall, respondents ranged from less than one year in the field to over 20 years.

2. *Type of position.* Fifty-four percent of the respondents were in-house trainers (compared to 71% in the previous year's survey), 21% were external providers (unchanged from the previous year), and 25% were in managerial positions (not accounted for in the previous year's survey).

3. *Internal populations.* The most frequent number of employees served by the survey respondents was greater than 2,000, most frequently with a staff of two to five employees to support training and development products and services within the organization.

4. *Looking to the future.* We asked the respondents to gaze into their crystal balls and compare the environment today (1997) with what they expect by the year 2000. Their questions addressed the following two areas:

   • Intranet and Internet use: Over the next three years, the survey respondents believe that companies will increasingly use technology for delivering training.

   • Outsourcing: There will be a moderate increase in outsourcing training to external providers over the next few years, and it remains a key concern for internal training professionals.

Analyzing the Data

Identifying and managing bias during the analysis will help you get the results that will lead to the right solution. Worksheet 3.1 will help you identify and manage the bias related to the data you gathered in step 2. In column 1, list the methods you used to gather the data. In columns 2 through 4, answer the questions for each of those methods.

Three major tasks are involved in analyzing the data: 1) sorting the data, 2) tabulating the data, and 3) comparing raw data with condensed data. Regardless of type of analysis used, analysis begins with sorting the data by respondent type, location, or some other identifying information. Sorting the data allows you to see if the information has been collected correctly. For example, if an online survey was used, you will see whether each survey is complete or completed correctly and what data needs to be excluded. Inaccurately completed surveys should be excluded from tabulation, as should incomplete interviews and observations.

Most inaccuracies in survey completion are caused by the respondent's misinterpretation of the directions. Sometimes interviews and observations cannot be completed because of some unforeseen problem at the time of the data collection; for example, the person being observed may be called away for an emergency or may experience extreme discomfort while being observed. Data from focus groups or job mapping sessions, however, is rarely excluded.

The sort will result in data that is grouped for tabulation. Data tabulation, perhaps the most tedious task associated with data analysis, is the extraction and categorization of data from the instruments you used to gather it that enables you to review and understand it. Data can be tabulated either manually or using a computer. For open-ended data, such as that resulting from interviews or focus groups, manual tabulation is most often used in completing a content analysis, although some sophisticated and costly software exists that can perform this task. Sometimes a key word search is conducted using a computer program. The tabulation of closed data like that from surveys is most quickly done by computer but can also be done by hand.

The goal of tabulation is to reduce data from its raw state into some type of quantified format without changing its meaning. Interpretation of the data cannot begin until it is tabulated and reduced. When you have condensed the raw data, you should compare it with the condensed data using one of the data comparison procedures listed in table 3.3 to ensure that the data has not been distorted.

Several off-the-shelf data analysis tools are available that may be useful in quickly completing your data analysis. Their producers' Websites were identified during a preliminary search of the marketplace, and not all have been used or tested by the authors.

Worksheet 3.1: Identifying Potential Data Biases

1 Data Collection Method Used	2 Who Collected the Data?	3 What Bias Exists?	4 How Can This Bias Be Managed?
Telephone interviews	Three members of the WLP team	Potential for leading the results to a classroom solution based on strong beliefs of one member of the team.	There is an approved script with pre-fixed probes. All team members follow the same script. Data is analyzed across the three interviewers to ensure that the trends are consistent and that, if a classroom trend exists, it has occurred in all three sets of interviews and not just the biased person's interviews.
		The requester will support only a solution that focuses on technical procedures and does not include soft skills training, even if needed to improve job performance.	The questions are designed and the analysis is positioned without a predisposition for any one content area.

The list provided in table 3.4 is a starting place, and we highly recommend that you conduct further research on these products to determine their usefulness for your data analysis.

Interpreting the Results

Once you are certain that the condensed data is stable (i.e., that it accurately reflects the raw data), you are ready to interpret it. Questions to ask related to each type of analysis are listed below to help you think through and plan for your data analysis. Worksheets 3.2, 3.3, and 3.4 were designed to help jump-start the interpretation of the data for each of the three methods of data analysis. Each worksheet poses several questions related to the analysis that will help you understand what the data is saying.

Content Analysis

- How can the data be coded so that it represents a category for data counts? For example, CP might refer to computer programs, or L might refer to leadership training.

- What is the meaning of the data, and what alternative meanings should be considered when reviewing the data?

- Is a reliable data pattern emerging, and if so, what is it?

Table 3.3: Data Comparison Procedures

Data Comparison Procedure	When to Use
Chronological arrangement	This procedure is particularly helpful when analyzing jobs or tasks. Arranging events in the order in which they happened or were observed is usually the simplest and most effective manner. Chronological arrangement also is useful in identifying when a performance problem began or in separating symptoms from the problem. For example, if you observe someone using a sales process and he or she does not overcome resistance when it first occurs, you get a big clue about what the problem is in closing sales. So you arrange the behavior or activities and outcomes chronologically.
Partition or division	Breaking data down into its parts and then studying the functions, relationships, or interdependencies of the parts often assists in understanding the whole. This ensures that the intervention designed explains the relationships so the audience understands why it is important to complete a certain step before initiating the next or not to take certain shortcuts on the system.
Cause and effect	Reviewing the data collected for causes and effects often identifies the factors that have the greatest impact on performance (e.g., in 90% of the cases when a salesperson did not overcome resistance early in the sales process, the sale did not close). Once the causes and effects have been identified from the data analysis, ordering them from most to least critical will usually prioritize recommendations or solutions.
Classification	Classifying data into like groups or similar content is often helpful in determining trends and validating similarities of data found across different methods. For example, the data from the survey supports the data from the focus group. Or, regardless of educational background, both the survey and focus group data shows a desire for simulations or hands-on training for the new computer system.

Table 3.4: Off-the-Shelf Data Analysis Tools

Data Analysis Company	Website Address
Survey Tracker	www.surveytracker.com
Question Mark	www.questionmark.com
SAS	www.sas.com
SPSS	www.spss.com
Excel	www.msn.com
Access	www.msn.com
WinCalc	www.adac.com
Analyze-it	www.analyze-it.com
CAQDAS	www.caqdas.soc.urregac.uk
QQQ Software	www.qqqsoft.com

Worksheet 3.2: Jump-Starting Content Analysis Interpretation

Content Analysis Consideration	What Does the Data Tell You?
What content consistently is repeated across groups?	
What content is specific to certain groups and is not universal?	
What content was mentioned infrequently, and by whom (demographics)?	
Does the data gathered establish trends for performance objectives? If so, what are the trends?	
Does the data gathered fall under specific topics? If so, what topics?	
What data is missing that was expected?	
Does the data establish trends for environmental barriers? If so, what are the barriers?	
Does the data establish trends for the performance problem and its causes? If so, what are they?	

Process Analysis

- What tools or support materials were used in completing the process? Was this use consistent across group members or specific to those new to the process or with much experience?
- What variables affected the process?
- What interdependencies exist in the data identified for the process?

Quantitative Analysis

- What data discrepancies exist, and how can they be accounted for?
- What relationships exist within the data?
- How can the data be measured (e.g., percentage, count, ratio)?

- What is missing from the data?
- What does the data mean: How would you interpret the results?
- What is the unit of analysis?
- Is the data reliable and predictable?

When you have finished interpreting the data and have the findings regarding the current situation, you will be ready to list the results by key findings. If you have used more than one method of analysis to arrive at these findings, it may be helpful to document the results using worksheet 3.5. The main categories for the key findings are listed in the column to the left, and sample key findings are listed in the middle column. Fill in your key findings in the right-hand column. These key findings will enable you to take the

---

Worksheet 3.3: Jump-Starting Process Analysis Interpretation

Process Analysis Consideration	What Does the Data Tell You?
What steps of the work process (for a specific job) are used most consistently across the audience?	
Does this process vary from location to location? If so, how does it vary, and why?	
Does the process vary from person to person? If so, how does it vary, and why?	
Does the data establish trends for the flow of work?	
Does the data establish trends for environmental barriers? If so, what are the barriers?	
Does the data establish trends for performance objectives? If so, what are the objectives?	
Does the data gathered fall under specific topics? If so, what topics?	
What data is missing that was expected?	

---

interpretation even further by comparing your analysis results with the business drivers and needs you identified in step 1.

Aligning Results with Business Drivers and Business Needs

Most of the hard work is now completed, but the most important work lies ahead. You must align the results of your analysis with the business drivers and needs you identified in step 1. This activity is critical, because eventually it will lead you to the solution that

will increase performance and meet the identified business need.

In step 1 of the Rapid Needs Analysis process you identified performance needs, business needs, and business drivers (worksheet 1.1) for the requested or potential solution. This told you how closely linked the solution was to the business and how realistic the solution might be in meeting the identified performance need. To get to the right solution, you will need to align these drivers and needs to your data analysis findings. The analysis findings should present a clear picture of the current situation, including the performance of the target audience, so that you can complete this alignment.

Worksheet 3.4: Jump-Starting Quantitative Analysis Interpretation

Quantitative Analysis Consideration	What Does the Data Tell You?
What do the numbers reveal about the audience demographics?	
Do the numbers point to any trends? If so, what trends?	
Does the data gathered establish trends for performance objectives? If so, what are the objectives?	
Does the data gathered fall under specific topics? If so, what topics?	
What data is missing that was expected?	

Worksheet 3.5: Current Situation Key Findings Worksheet

Key Findings Category	Sample Key Findings	Your Key Findings
Findings regarding the request	The request was to identify the specifics for a new sales process that would increase sales counselors' sales results. The findings, however, reveal that the organization needs to focus on other things first, such as identifying clear performance objectives, developing a consistent performance development process, and training its supervisors to be proficient in the skills required by the sales counselors and coaching skills.	
Organizational findings	There are no clear objectives set at the corporate level to direct the expected performance. Performance development is an arbitrary activity and is not performed consistently. Supervisors are deficient in sales skills and competitor information and cannot provide the coaching that is needed.	

Worksheet 3.5: Current Situation Key Findings Worksheet (continued)

Key Findings Category	Sample Key Findings	Your Key Findings
Environmental findings	The customer information file is outdated. Every customer contact employee has a personal computer at his or her desk.	
Audience skill level	Sales counselors are deficient in cross-selling skills. Sales counselors are proficient in closing the sales when the customer requests a specific product.	
Audience knowledge level	Sales counselors understand the company's products to the extent that they can identify products requested by customers. Sales counselors do not know major competitors' products.	
Audience performance level	Sales counselors are not addressing customer questions about the competition. Sales counselors are losing sales opportunities. Sales counselors on average have a 1.1 cross-sales ratio. Sales counselors are not using customer information during sales interactions.	
Audience perceptions	Sales counselors are confused about the need for a new sales process and a new system. Sales counselors believe they are doing a good job considering the support they receive and the lack of clarity that exists about what they are supposed to do.	
Best practice findings	Best practices regarding successful sales process training include the following: • Clear performance objectives are in place. • Performance development processes exist and are consistent. • Supervisors are trained in sales skills. • Supervisors are trained in coaching skills. • Sales performance is measured. • Above-average sales performance is recognized and rewarded. • Communication programs send key messages on a daily basis.	

(continued on next page)

Worksheet 3.5: Current Situation Key Findings Worksheet (continued)

Key Findings Category	Sample Key Findings	Your Key Findings
Measurement, results, and outcomes findings	Sales performance is measured inconsistently from office to office and sometimes person to person.	
	Sales counselors are not motivated to improve their performance.	
	Confusion exists among the audience regarding what they should focus on; one day it is selling product X, and the next day the focus is on product Y.	
	The sales reports are hard to read, and the information is old and often inaccurate.	
	Measures are not related to performance expectations.	

Worksheet 3.6 will assist you in completing this alignment. In the left-hand column, note the key findings from your data analysis. Then note the identified solution in column 2 and the performance needs in column 3. Next, align the business needs and drivers that you identified in step 1 in columns 4 and 5 as they correspond to the findings, solution, and performance needs. The worksheet contains an example of results that are aligned with business needs and drivers.

Worksheet 3.7 duplicates the business need and driver from the previous worksheet; however, the findings do not align with them. The findings of the analysis reveal that the sales counselors' performance is very good, which means they are not the problem and another solution needs to be investigated.

What you should know after completing this alignment is whether the current situation, if remedied, will support the business need. If you discover a misalignment among the data findings, the identified solution, the performance needs, and the business drivers and needs, then you may have to go back to step 1 and validate the business needs and drivers with the requester, sponsor, and others. Or you may have to revisit the data analysis to make certain it was conducted correctly. In any event, you should not proceed with validating or recommending a solution until the data findings, identified solution, performance needs, and business drivers and needs are in sync.

Identifying the Performance Gap

The *performance gap* is the difference between the expected or required performance or outcomes and the current performance that you identified through the data analysis. By determining or validating a performance gap, you will be able to compare the other data gathered against this gap to determine if a recommended solution will indeed close it. In other words, will the solution bring the current performance up to or proficient with the expected performance? This activity can be seen as insurance that the solution responds to the expected outcomes identified by managers in step 1 of the Rapid Needs Analysis process. It will help you quickly validate the requested or potential solution or recommend another, more effective solution.

To identify the performance gap, list the expected performance and the data analysis findings relating to current performance and determine the difference between the two. Worksheet 3.8 is provided as a template to get you started in this activity.

Worksheet 3.6: Aligning Results with Business Needs and Drivers —Aligned Example

Data Analysis Key Finding	Identified Solution	Performance Needs	Business Need	Business Driver
Sales counselors are not addressing customer questions about the competition. Sales counselors are losing sales opportunities. Sales counselors on average have a 1.1 cross-sales ratio. Sales counselors are not using customer information during sales interactions.	Comprehensive sales training	Increase sales counselors' ability to • sell against competition • cross sell • use customer information	To increase presence in the market because key competitors are offering products in new markets on an ongoing basis.	Loss of market share (competition—external driver)

Evaluating the Identified Solution

You have completed the majority of activities for data analysis. You have planned the analysis, identified data bias, chosen the analysis methods to use, analyzed the data, interpreted the results, aligned the results with the business drivers and needs, and identified or validated the performance gap. The purpose of the remaining activities is to ensure that the solution you ultimately recommend and implement will provide the desired results. Worksheet 3.9 will help you validate the identified solution by identifying each data analysis criterion, the data that should come from the analysis for that criterion, and the key findings and relationship to the solution for that criterion. An example of how to complete the first analysis criterion is provided in the worksheet.

Identifying Performance Measures

At this point in the Rapid Needs Analysis process, it is important to identify measures that will be used to evaluate the solution's success. These measures

Worksheet 3.7: Aligning Results with Business Needs and Drivers —Nonaligned Example

Data Analysis Key Finding	Identified Solution	Performance Needs	Business Need	Business Driver
Sales counselors are addressing customer questions about the competition. Sales counselors on average are closing 90% of all sales. Sales counselors on average have a 3.8 cross-sales ratio. Sales counselors are routinely using customer information during sales interactions.	Comprehensive sales training	Increase sales counselors' ability to • sell against competition • cross sell • use customer information	To increase presence in the market because key competitors are offering products in new markets on an ongoing basis.	Loss of market share (competition—external driver)

should link to the business drivers, business needs, and expected performance.

Identifying measures as early as possible in the process will enable you to discover information that is important to the design and development of the solution as well as the evaluation of its success. Identifying measures will further validate the solution by linking it back to the business factors driving the solution and the performance that should result.

The measures that will be most meaningful must be based on and relate to the business drivers, business needs, and expected performance identified in step 1. This will ensure that the measures will evaluate what is important to the organization. Table 3.5 is an example of how measures link to business drivers, business needs, and expected performance.

For more information about how to identify performance measures, please refer to *Rapid Evaluation,* the first book of the ASTD Learning and Performance Workbook Series. Chapter 2, "Establishing Measures," addresses how to identify measures to use in evaluating a WLP strategy or intervention. It describes how to validate business drivers and performance needs and identify measures from those needs. Also addressed is how to determine a measurement approach and identify issues and concerns regarding measurement. How to

Worksheet 3.8: Identifying the Performance Gap

Expected Performance	Current Performance	The Gap	How Will Requested or Potential Solution Close the Gap?
Proactively cross-sell based on customer needs to increase the number of products sold per customer resulting in a departmental cross-sales ratio of 3.0	Customers are purchasing one product per sales encounter, most of the time because the customer requested that product. The department's cross-sales ratio is 1.0, far below the industry standard.	Sales counselors are not recommending products based on customers' needs. Sales counselors are not familiar with the organization's or competitors' products. Sales counselors are not familiar with which products complement each other, which would make it easier for them to sell a combination package. Cross-sales results are lacking by two percentage points.	The comprehensive sales training course will close the gap by providing company and competitor product knowledge, sales skills, and referral skills that will enable the sales counselor to increase the number of products sold per customer at one time.

determine the intensity of the measures used in evaluation and how to align measures with the objectives of an evaluation strategy or intervention are also addressed.

Validating the Identified Solution with Requester, Sponsor, and Stakeholders

The last activity in step 3 of the Rapid Needs Analysis process is validating the identified solution with the requester, sponsor, and stakeholders. At this point it is critical to condense all of the information you have into a short report that makes a strong and compelling case for your recommendation. The report should be no more than three pages in length and should highlight what led you to recommend the solution. The information that should be included in this report includes the following:

- the requested or potential solution
- the reason for conducting the needs analysis
- who was involved in the analysis
- the methods used and why
- key findings by method

Worksheet 3.9: Solution Evaluation Criteria

Analysis Criterion	Data Related to Criterion	Key Findings and the Relationship to the Solution
What is the business problem to be resolved by the solution?	Example: A new system is being developed for monitoring employee performance and "paying for performance."	Example: Audience perception of the system is that it will limit their pay, so the solution must sell them on the system. Example: Performance standards are not in place, although the new system provides an evaluation against standards.
What is the business problem to be resolved by the solution?		
What are the expected outcomes?		
What are the processes that support or affect job performance related to the business problem?		
What is the problem with the performance of the job?		
Is the problem related to a knowledge or skill deficiency?		
Are there other performers who affect or support the output of the performer? Who are they?		
What are the standards and references for the performance criteria?		
Who is the target audience for the solution?		
What is the mix of experience, job positions, and education in the audience?		
How familiar are audience members with each other? Is this important?		
What is the motivation for the audience to improve the performance or resolve the problem or meet the business need?		
Are there special needs that should be considered? Are they integrated into the solution?		

Table 3.5: Linking Business Drivers, Business Needs, and Expected Performance to Measures

Business Driver	Business Need	Expected Performance	Measure
Loss of market share (competition—external)	To increase presence in the market because key competitors are offering products in new markets on an ongoing basis.	Sales counselors will cross-sell based on customer needs to increase the number of products sold per sales session, resulting in a departmental cross-sales ratio of 3.0.	Cross-sales ratio (number of products sold per each customer contact) Closed referrals (number of products sold based on referrals) Account retention (number of accounts remaining active over a set period of time)

- conclusions based on data interpretation
- how findings align with business drivers and needs
- the performance gap
- how the identified solution closes the gap
- performance measures for the solution.

The information contained in the report is best delivered in person, but there are other ways it can be reported effectively. The most frequently used alternative methods of presenting the analysis findings are Webshops, which are interactive sessions conducted over the Web that most often use PowerPoint slides to guide the discussion, and telephone conferences, for which slides should be sent beforehand for use during the discussion.

To be adequately prepared to present your findings and recommendation to the requester, sponsor, and stakeholders, you must not only have thorough knowledge of the content of the report, but also anticipate how the recommended solution will be received, including potential objections and resistance. Some things to consider before delivering the results and recommendation include the following:

- What are the issues surrounding the development of the identified solution?
- How could you deal with these issues?
- How well will the identified solution meet the business need and provide the expected outcomes?
- What is the biggest weakness of the solution?
- What could you do to offset or overcome this weakness?
- What will you do if you are unable to validate the solution with the requester, sponsor, and stakeholders?

Having answers to these questions will help you deal with problems in validating the recommended solution and gaining commitment to moving forward with the solution's design and development.

Chapter Summary

In this chapter, step 3 of the Rapid Needs Analysis process was introduced and discussed. Case examples of how various organizations used the three types of data analysis methods covered were provided. How to plan for the data analysis, choose data analysis methods, identify data bias, and analyze and interpret data was covered. Information on how to align the results of the analysis with the business; identify a performance gap; validate the requested or potential solution or recommend another solution; identify performance measures; and validate the recommended solution with the requester, sponsor, and stakeholders was also included in this chapter.

Discussion Questions

The following questions are provided to help you apply what you learned in this chapter:

- What is one benefit of planning the analysis before diving into it?

- What data analysis methods do you think you will use for your data analysis, and why?

- What data bias might you encounter during your data analysis?

- What three tasks are involved in analyzing the data?

- How can you jump-start the interpretation of the data?

- Why is it important to align the results with the business drivers and business needs?

- What is a performance gap, and why do you need to identify it at this point in the needs analysis?

- What is the importance of evaluating the identified solution before identifying performance measures and validating it with others?

- Why should you identify performance measures at this point in the process?

- What information should you review with your requester, sponsor, and stakeholders, and how can you plan for dealing with objections or resistance to the recommended solution?

4

Step 4: Determining Solution Specifications

In step 4 of the Rapid Needs Analysis process you will determine specifications, resources, and costs for the identified solution. This activity speeds development of the solution by immediately translating the analysis findings into design and development requirements. It also prepares you to identify the risks and benefits involved in developing and implementing the solution and to seek approval for doing so.

At the end of step 4 you will have identified

- the detailed specifications for your solution
- how these specifications will lead to the solution's success
- the resources required for developing and implementing the solution
- the costs associated with the required resources
- the risks and benefits of the solution.

Determining specifications at this point will ensure that the solution is the correct one, will decrease the potential for mistakes that could result in re-work or other costly remedies, and will link the analysis to the outcomes identified by the requester. During step 4, analysis and solution development begin to overlap. What once was seen as a purely development activity is now considered an analysis activity that quickly and accurately facilitates decisions about how (and if) the solution should be developed.

What Are Solution Specifications?

Solution specifications are best defined as a detailed description of what will make the solution successful in meeting business needs, meeting performance needs, and closing the performance gap. Think of these specifications as a detailed and precise plan for developing the solution. By identifying the specifications, you will have all the information you need to complete a design document or blueprint for the development of the solution. Table 4.1 lists the most

typical solution specifications and defines what needs to be identified for each specification.

Case Examples

Specifications are determined most often in two ways: during face-to-face meetings or through electronic means. The following case examples discuss how two companies with different needs determined specifications using each of these methods.

Case Example 1

A financial institution with a strong regional presence conducted a needs analysis for an electronic performance support system (EPSS) for a customer call center whose employees answered customer questions and sold complementary products. The EPSS was intended to provide consistent, up-to-the-minute customer, product, and competitor information. The expected outcomes of the solution were to increase sales and profitability, to decrease customer complaints, and to increase employee satisfaction.

The WLP manager who conducted the analysis decided that the specifications should be determined by sales managers, systems managers, operations managers, training managers, select regional managers, key developers, and programmers. Further, he decided that an in-person, facilitated meeting would quickly get to the specifications. Because of the enormity of the system conversion and the degree of change to the environment, he felt it would be worth the expense to bring everyone together in one place at one time to determine specifications. Additionally, once validated and translated into resource and cost needs, the specifications would immediately be transferred to screen prototypes, thus decreasing the time needed to develop the solution.

During the two-day in-person meeting, first the purpose, roles, and responsibilities involved in determining specifications were communicated. Next, the findings of the needs analysis were presented and discussed, and finally the group determined the specifications.

Because the requester and key stakeholders were part of the group determining the specifications, a final decision was made at the end of the meeting, and no further validation was needed. Following the meeting,

Table 4.1: Solution Specifications

Solution Specification Category	What Needs to Be Identified
Scope	What is the size of the solution (its breadth and depth)?
	How complex does the content need to be?
	How many components will make up the solution?
	How much information, or what depth of knowledge or skills, is required to meet the business and performance needs?
	How many other groups, processes, or systems interface with this solution, and how should they be integrated into the solution?
Delivery method or media	How complex does the method or media need to be?
	Will training or development be needed for the designers to use the method or media?
	Will the method or media rely on others to be effective (e.g., information systems must provide computer network support)?
	What is the average time to design or develop a product using this type of method or media?
Format and look	How must the solution look (e.g., does a job aid need to fit on a desk, or should it be an electronic tool)?
	How must the solution be formatted (e.g., does it need to fit in a calendar, or must it conform to Word for Windows 2000)?
Content	What are the knowledge requirements?
	What are the skill requirements?
	Will the content be conceptual, experiential, or cognitive?
	How intense does the content need to be?
	Will the content require extensive knowledge or experience?
	How much content must be delivered?
	Will content development be dependent on subject matter experts?
Outcomes or results	Is the desired result to have an awareness of the subject matter?
	Is the desired result to be able to transfer the subject matter back to the job and have a business process or financial impact?
	Are the outcomes or results expected from the solution key to the organization's short- or long-term strategy?
	Do the expected results affect the feasibility of a major company initiative?
Audience	Is the audience well versed in the content of the solution?
	Is the audience willing and ready to implement the solution?
	Is the audience's environment conducive to implementing the solution?

Table 4.1: Solution Specifications (continued)

Solution Specification Category	What Needs to Be Identified
Business impact	How critical is this solution to the organization?
	If the solution is not successful or needs to be re-worked or refined, what will the impact be on the business need or performance need?
	Does this performance need affect only one business area, or does it affect more than one area? To what extent is the overall business affected by the need?
	Does the business or performance need that this solution addresses involve the bread and butter of the company?
	Is the solution needed to meet a contract obligation or support a product rollout?
Experience, education, or other prerequisites	If a prerequisite has been identified, is information about it available? Is it also in development?
	How does this solution fit in an employee's development plan?
	Will this solution stand alone?
Sources to use for development	Are subject matter experts available who can supply or validate the content? Who are they?
	Does documentation exist or are resources available that should be used in the development of the solution?
Content supplements	In addition to the identified deliverables, will anything else be used to supplement the content when the individual returns to the job (e.g., system or procedural manuals, supervisor authority)?
	How should these supplements be reflected in the content?
	What is the stability of the supplemental information?
Related processes or interdependencies	What are the related interdependencies for this material (e.g., sales process, procurement process, system procedures, incentive plan)?
	Who owns the related processes, and how should this information be reflected in the content (e.g., as a reference, as a section of the content)?
	What is the accuracy and stability of the related information?

the WLP manager identified the resources, costs, benefits, and risks of not developing the solution and presented the solution to the sponsor for approval. The needs assessment and creation of the specifications, from start to finish, took two weeks to complete.

Case Example 2

A worldwide provider of computer training identified the need to upgrade its delivery system to include Web-based training to its external customers around the world. A needs analysis was conducted to determine if the solution was needed and, if so, to determine how it should be done. The analysis resulted in conclusions and recommendations that were the basis of specifications for the new system of delivery.

The delivery manager who conducted the analysis decided that the specifications should be determined by a group including stakeholders (project managers, product managers, and country managers), subject matter experts who had knowledge of the content, solution developers including programmers and Web experts, and regional managers and trainers. Because those involved in determining the specifications were located in many countries and were familiar with using technology in decision making, and because the company valued including as many people in this process as possible, a virtual (electronic) war room was used. (*War rooms,* a method for gathering the details needed to design and develop a solution without facilitation, are described later in this chapter.) Before setting up the war room, the project manager communicated the purpose, roles, and responsibilities involved in determining specifications and discussed the findings of the needs analysis in a two-hour Webcast.

The virtual war room was available for one week to accommodate the participants' varying schedules and time available to devote to determining the specifications. After the week was up, the project manager responsible for completing the analysis reviewed and condensed the potential specifications. She then met for two hours (again via Webcast) with project, product, and country managers to finalize and validate the specifications. The specifications were determined in a little more than one week and represented the thoughts and opinions of key players from every country.

The project manager was then able to identify the resources needed and their cost, as well as the benefits and risks involved in not moving forward with the solution. Once she presented all the necessary information, she was able to gain approval from the project sponsor, who was the manager of worldwide customer training.

Step 4 Activities

There are nine activities to complete in step 4 of the Rapid Needs Analysis process:

1. identifying who will be involved in determining specifications
2. communicating purpose, roles, and responsibilities
3. discussing needs analysis findings
4. determining the specifications
5. finalizing and validating the specifications
6. identifying resources needed to develop and implement the solution
7. identifying the costs associated with the solution
8. identifying the risks versus the benefits of the solution
9. gaining sponsor approval to proceed with developing the solution.

Identifying Who Will Be Involved in Determining Specifications

Involving your stakeholders, subject matter experts, solution designers, and to a lesser extent managers and supervisors (and perhaps a small sampling of the target audience) is important in determining the specifications for the identified solution. These people hold the key to the information that will unlock the specifics of what will make the solution successful. Keep in mind that many of these people will also be involved in the development of the solution, so this is a good time to recruit those who you think will be able to provide information and guidance throughout the design and development process. Table 4.2 lists the

Table 4.2: Typical Specification Determination Participants

Type of Participant	Rationale for Involvement
Stakeholders	Stakeholders have the most to gain from the business outcome of the performance improvement that the solution will provide. The key responsibility of the stakeholder is to ensure that the solution links to the business need.
Subject matter experts	Subject matter experts are responsible for providing content information including processes, procedures, and environmental data so that the specifications result in a solution that will close the performance gap.
Solution designers	This team is responsible for designing and developing the solution based on the identified specifications. Team members may be internal or external and may include systems employees (if needed), designers, and writers.
Managers and supervisors	Managers and supervisors of those participating in the solution are responsible for ensuring that the content of the solution being developed will close the performance gap.
Participants	Participants will participate in the solution once it is developed. A few members of this group may be involved in determining the specifics to ensure that the solution fits the audience's and environmental needs.

people who most typically will be involved in this activity and the rationale for involving them.

Having the right participants in solution specification is critical to the accuracy of the output of this step in the process and will contribute enormously to the speed with which the specifications can be translated into a design document and then developed into a successful solution. A major consideration in choosing the "right" person is ensuring that whomever you select has the expertise needed to determine the specifications for the identified solution. In table 4.3 the most common types of solutions are listed in the first column, and the questions you should ask in identifying who should be involved in determining the specifications are listed in the second column. The answers to these questions should point you to the people who will provide the best specifications.

Table 4.3: Identifying Whom to Involve in Determining Specifications

Type of Solution	Questions to Help You Identify Who Should be Involved
Process change (e.g., sales training, procurement training, operations training, telephone center, order intake, customer service)	Who is responsible for the development of the process? Who will be most affected by the process (e.g., customers, accounting)? Who is documenting the process change? Who is responsible for the output of the process change (e.g., marketing, procurement, call center management)? Who determined the original need for the process change?
Skill development (e.g., leadership training, management development, customer satisfaction skills, negotiation, interviewing skill)	Who identified the original skill development need, and why? Who is considered an expert in the skill? Who will be responsible for transferring the skills back on the job?
New system or systems conversion (e.g., operations system, human resources system, payroll system, new accounts system, customer information system, accounting system, electronic performance support system, medical records)	Who is developing the system? Are there procedures that will support the system, and if so, who is authoring the procedures? Who is writing the test scripts for the system? Who championed the system originally? Who will be ultimately responsible for the outcomes of the system once it is implemented?
Technical training (e.g., regulations, required training for certifications, specific training for jobs, procedural training)	Who has information about the technical training requirements? Who is the key contact for the technical information? Who is responsible for the outcomes of the training? What business unit (e.g., accounting, human resources) is championing the change or need for training? Who will be affected by the ultimate information (e.g., customers for order taking)?
Job aid (e.g., electronic system, code card for use with customer, product information)	Who ultimately is responsible for the work that relates to the job aid? Who will use the job aid? Who will supply the information for the job aid? Is there a graphic specialist or other design expert that can provide information on layout and design?

In thinking about who you will involve in determining the specifications for the solution, keep the following in mind:

- Is the person motivated to participate in this activity? Why or why not?

- Will he or she take the time to participate? Why or why not?

- Does the person have information, expertise, and experience that will lead to a meaningful contribution?

- How well does the person work as part of a team?

- Is there any reason not to involve this person in determining the specifications for the solution?

Communicating Purpose, Roles, and Responsibilities

To garner their support, you should follow certain steps before meeting with those who will be involved in determining the specifications for the solution.

First, communicate the purpose of determining the specifications for the solution. You should communicate the following about the purpose to those involved:

- *Solution specifications* are best defined as a detailed description of what will make the solution successful in meeting business needs, meeting performance needs, and closing the performance gap.

- Solution specifications will provide the foundation for how the solution will be developed.

- Determining specifications will ensure that the solution is correct, help avoid mistakes that could result in re-work or other costly remedies, and increase the likelihood that the solution will provide the outcomes identified by the requester.

- Solution specifications will result in a detailed and precise plan for what will be developed.

Second, communicate each person's role and responsibilities and the benefits of being involved. It's a good idea to be explicit about why you want them involved and what's in it for them. Points to communicate include the following:

- The value you see them bringing to the activity is usually related to their expertise or role within the organization. Stakeholder involvement ensures that business needs will be met through the solution. Subject matter expert involvement ensures that the correct information is used to develop the solution. Manager and supervisor involvement ensures that the performance gap closes. Participant involvement ensures that the right knowledge and skills are developed.

- What you want those involved in the process to do is to identify specifications for the identified solution from the point of view of their expertise or role (see table 4.2).

- What most participants will get out of their involvement will be assurance that the solution is the right one and that it is developed and implemented quickly.

Third, communicate how much time will be needed for this process and where and how the specification determination will take place. The first time requirement will be to attend a meeting (no more than two hours in length) conducted in person or via telephone conference or Webcast. The purpose of this meeting is to discuss the needs analysis findings and to enable participants to ask questions about the findings and how they relate to the development of the solution. The findings will in large part provide the information that shapes the specifications.

The next time requirement is the actual determination of the specifications. The time needed for this determination varies depending on the scope of the solution to be developed and the process used to determine the specifications. For example, an in-person, facilitated meeting may take from two hours to two days to complete, depending on the scope of the solution. If the solution has been identified as a paper-based job aid, it will probably take no more than two hours to determine the specifications. However, if the solution is a comprehensive EPSS, two days probably will be required. Time requirements will be addressed in more depth later in this chapter.

Specification determination can happen with everyone involved at one time in the same room, or it can happen in a virtual environment. It can be facilitated or nonfacilitated. How it is done depends greatly on the people and politics involved and the way the organization conducts decision-making processes. This, too, will be addressed in more detail later in this chapter.

Discussing Needs Analysis Findings

Discussing the needs analysis findings with those who will determine the specifications for the solution is an important step in this process. Many of the people who will be involved in the determination were not involved in the analysis or were not privy to the report of findings, and as a result they have not had an opportunity to ask questions about what the findings mean. Knowledge of the results of the analysis will increase the value of their contribution enormously, because they will understand the rationale for the selection of the solution.

This discussion can be conducted in person or via telephone conference or Webcast. The way the meeting is conducted is largely a function of what is accepted in the company for this type of information dissemination and question-and-answer session.

Discussion participants must use the findings of the needs analysis to provide the details needed to develop the solution. They will look at the key findings from the analysis, link those findings to specific recommendations, and then add more detail to the recommendations for the solution. The specifications should include how the solution will look (in other words, its visual format), how it will be structured, how it will be delivered (through what media), who will deliver it, and how environmental or equipment needs will be addressed.

Table 4.4 shows how one company translated needs analysis findings into solution specifications. You can use the same grid to translate your findings into specifications. The conclusions resulting from the analysis should be listed in the first column, the recommendations related to the conclusions listed in the middle column, and the related solution specifications listed in the third column. The worksheet example is only a partial listing of the specifications needed for the solution identified, computer training in Office 2000.

Determining the Specifications

Now that preparations have been completed, the next activity in step 4 is to actually determine the specifications for the solution. This activity can take place during an extension of the discussion meeting described above or separately. The format can be tra-

ditional face-to-face facilitated meetings or Webcasts or, more creatively, nonfacilitated virtual or physical war rooms.

Facilitated Face-to-Face Meetings or Webcasts

Facilitated face-to-face meetings are the most prevalent format for determining solution specifications. In this type of meeting a facilitator leads the group through the process of identifying the specifications, finding by finding and recommendation by recommendation.

Face-to-face meetings can get to the specifications quickly because all of the people involved in the determination are present at one time. Everyone's ideas and opinions are made public, and consensus is usually reached during the meeting. Consensus, of course, depends on the skill of the facilitator, who must lead the group to decisions and negotiate differences of opinion as they occur.

Some tips for planning this type of meeting are as follows:

- Recruit (either from within or outside the department or company) a skilled facilitator who is not a stakeholder in the solution.
- Prepare the facilitator by reviewing the needs analysis findings and how these findings lead to determining the specifications.
- With the facilitator, identify processes for getting to the specifications and handling differences of opinion and disagreement.
- Prepare and publish an agenda for the session that specifies participant expectations. If this meeting is held at the same time as the meeting to communicate the purpose, roles, and responsibilities involved in determining specifications, then it is important that this agenda be sent prior to that meeting.
- Prepare the "specification topic boards" prior to the meeting (whether in-person or Web based). Specification boards are described later in this chapter.

War Rooms

War rooms have been used in product design and rapid prototyping for many years. In its original context, a war room is a place where military moves are simulated to test the validity of military theory, the

Table 4.4: Translating Needs Analysis Findings into Solution Specifications (Identified Solution: Training for Office 2000)

Needs Analysis Conclusions	Related Needs Analysis Recommendations	Related Solution Specifications and Categories
Over two thirds of the audience is not proficient in using computer programs for calculating interest rates or in performing other complex calculations that are important to their sales and services results.	A computer training program that uses all functions of Office 2000 should be delivered to the audience in a classroom setting. Windows basics should be a self-study module that precedes the Office 2000 training.	The training will consist of two major components: 1. a self-study computer-based training module that supports learning the basic functions of Windows 2000 2. a classroom hands-on training in Office 2000 that integrates how to use the computer. (scope, delivery method or media, content, experience)
Most of the target audience do not have computers at their workstations and have not had any computer training except for Word.	Computer upgrades need to be made available for the target audience.	Computers need to be updated for every audience member's workstation prior to the classroom training. (scope, delivery method or media, experience)
The managers and supervisors are not proficient in using computer programs for calculating interest rates or in performing other complex calculations and are not able to provide on-the-job instruction or coaching to the audience.	Managers and supervisors need to take the same training and should be trained in coaching the required performance.	Managers and supervisors will take this training and will also take a coaching class that will prepare them to support the expected performance back on the job. The latter will be hands-on classroom training. (scope, content, outcomes or results, experience)
There are approximately 500 members of this audience located in six western states who need to be trained by the end of the next quarter.	To accommodate time and travel constraints, the training will need to take place in regions within each state.	An in-house technical training team that will be trained by external subject matter experts will conduct the classroom training. External experts will be present at the training to answer questions and troubleshoot. (delivery method or media)

quality of training, and the effectiveness of equipment. In the needs analysis context, a war room is a place where the details needed to design and develop a solution are planned without facilitation.

This method involves dedicating a room, either physical or virtual (such as a dedicated Website) where the people responsible for determining the specifications come and go as they please to add their thoughts and comments to specification topic boards. The idea is that those involved will provide their ideas, but also comment on what others have added to the boards in the process of getting to the "right" specifications.

The room is reserved for a set period of time. For a solution that is complicated and involves many different components, the room could be set up for as long as 10 days. For a simple solution, the room may be needed for one or two days at most. Most often, war rooms are active for three to five days. At the end of the set time, the information is recorded and sent electronically to all those involved, who then have an opportunity to review the specifications and offer comments or make changes one last time.

The benefits of determining solution specifications in this way are information that is not filtered or censored because of "what other people will think" and participants' ability to go back to the room as often as desired within the given time frame to continue to brainstorm ideas. The success of this method depends on setting ground rules for participation in advance and on selecting the "right" people to be involved. Because this method is not facilitated, it is important to choose people who are highly motivated to provide their ideas and opinions and who will do so independently, without prodding.

A few ground rules for implementing both physical and virtual war rooms should be communicated to those involved:

- Identify who has access to the room and why, and why others do not.

- Be specific about what you want comments on and what you do not. For example, if you know that the program has to run on Windows, state that the specifications should not address the operating system.

- Instruct participants to identify themselves as the authors of their comments so that if questions arise, participants can contact each other.

- Instruct participants to build on each other's ideas.

- Remind participants to comment on each other's ideas, but to avoid using inflammatory words when doing so (see table 4.5).

Figure 4.1 is a sample of a specification board that can be used in a virtual or physical war room or in a face-to-face meeting. One conclusion and its supporting recommendation are listed at the top of each board, and the potential specification categories (see table 4.1) are listed in the body of the board with room left for participants to write their comments. In a virtual war room, the boards are available electronically, and people can access the information as often as they like for a set period of time. Not all the specification

Table 4.5: Virtual War Room Guidelines

Guideline	Purpose
Determine if virtual war room technology is available in the organization.	If the technology is not available, you will not be able to conduct virtual war rooms without going to great expense.
Determine if the organization's culture supports the use of virtual war rooms.	If the culture values face-to-face interaction more than virtual interaction, this method may take more time in the long run.
Identify what needs to be placed on the Website.	To provide the Website administrators with the information they need to define the technological requirements of the war room
Identify participants and who has access to the room and why.	To ensure the right people participate in identifying solution specifications
Identify how participants should access and use Website.	To communicate how they use the technology to participate in solution specification
Identify how long war room will be available.	So participants can plan for their involvement
Define participant roles and responsibilities.	So participants will know their role in identifying solution specifications and exactly what they are supposed to do to identify them
Define expected results.	So participants understand the end result of their efforts
Specify what you want comments on and why.	To ensure you get the information needed to get to expected results
Instruct participants to identify their comments.	So others can contact them if they have questions about their comments
Instruct participants to build on each others' ideas.	To get to the "right" specifications
Remind participants to comment on each others' ideas but avoid inflammatory words when doing so.	To ensure that this is a good experience for everyone involved and that participants will be motivated to identify solution specifications in the future

categories will be applicable to all conclusions and recommendations, and therefore the example in figure 4.1 has some categories left blank.

Choosing the Specification Determination Method

The method you choose for determining the specifications depends on your needs and what will work well with the needs, culture, and politics of the organization. It also depends on how big the specification determination group is and where members are located.

For example, generating ideas and making decisions electronically might be business as usual for some organizations. Even if it takes a while longer to come to decisions using this method, it is a cultural norm. Electronic means to determine specifications are often used when those involved are located in faraway regions and it is perceived as important that all regions are represented.

On the other hand, if the solution is big enough and is a requirement, results are needed fast, and the organization values face-to-face interaction and consensus building, then a face-to face meeting will probably work best. You will be able to deal with differences of opinion and disagreements during the meeting and come to decisions quickly.

It is possible to use a combination of methods, but again this depends on the time you have available, the importance of the solution, and what the organizational culture will accept. We have worked with clients who have conducted virtual war rooms to include a wide audience of specification determiners and then conducted a face-to-face meeting with a small group to determine the final specifications. If a combination of methods is used, it is important to communicate the specific role of each group, the reasons for conducting the determination in this way, and the value of everyone's involvement.

Finalizing and Validating the Specifications

Before validating the specifications, you will need to document and, in some cases, finalize them. If you have reached final determinations through an in-person or Webcast meeting, then you must condense and document the specifications. If you used a war room, you will need to document the findings and present your recommendation for a final decision to those who will validate the specifications.

At this point in step 4 you are ready to validate the specifications with the requester (and potentially key stakeholders) to make sure the specifications will meet the original request or performance problem and the identified business need. You will need to include key stakeholders in this validation if, through the needs analysis and specification determination, you discover that the solution is more complex or bigger than the original request. If this occurs, the identified solution now involves other requesters (the stakeholders), who in a sense become co-owners of the solution. It is critical for them to be involved in the validation, because the solution must also meet their performance problems and business needs. Keep in mind that sometimes the requester is the sponsor or there is shared ownership for the solution among a group such as an advisory board.

Validation is most often conducted in a face-to-face meeting, but, depending on the location of those involved or the time and expense involved in traveling to a physical meeting site, a telephone conference or Webcast may suffice. These alternatives to an in-person meeting will work as long as the specifications are available for prior review along with samples of how the solution might look. These samples are helpful in giving the validators an idea of how the specifications will be developed into the solution.

In validating the solution specifications it is important to do the following three activities:

1. *Present the specifications for each conclusion and recommendation resulting from the needs analysis.* This presentation usually provides a summary of the specification boards for each conclusion and its supporting recommendations.

2. *Use samples or prototypes to illustrate what the specifications mean and how, when developed, they will look.* This helps those who are not in the WLP field "see" what the finished product will look like so that later they will not say, "That's not what I thought it would be."

3. *Align the specifications with the business drivers, business needs, expected performance, performance gap, and means of closing the gap, all of which you identified earlier in the Rapid Needs Analysis process.* Depending on how complex the solution is, you can do this alignment with those who are validating the specifications as a final checkpoint that they indeed are correct.

Worksheet 4.1 can be used in this alignment. The business drivers are listed in the first column. In the second column, each driver is linked to the resulting business need; and in column 3, the expected

Figure 4.1: Specification Board Sample
(Identified Solution: Training for Office 2000)

Conclusion:

Approximately 500 members of the identified audience (loan processors) located in six western states need to be trained by the end of the next quarter. It is critical that the audience is trained quickly and at minimum expense.

Recommendation:

The training should take place regionally in each state and be conducted by a training team who will be selected from the identified audience.

Potential Specifications by Category:

Scope

500 loan processors will be trained in two months in each region.

Delivery Method or Media

Subject matter experts will train the identified trainers. (ST)

Professional trainers will train the identified trainers. (JM)

The training team will consist of selected audience members and subject matter experts. (EK)

Criteria should be determined for selecting the audience training team. (JM)

The audience training team should self-select. (FV)

Managers and supervisors should conduct the training. (ST)

The self-study will be delivered by computer-based training. (ROL)

The bulk of the content will be delivered in a classroom setting. (ST)

Format and look

Content

Outcomes or results

Audience

Business impact

Experience, education, or other prerequisites

performance that will meet the business need is identified. In column 4, the performance gap is identified, along with how the solution will close it. Finally, in column 5, the specifications relating to each business driver, business need, expected performance, and performance gap are identified.

Completing this worksheet most likely will be your last checkpoint to ensure that the analysis findings align with the solution specifications and that they fit with the identified business and performance needs. The question to ask at this point is, Will the specifications result in a solution that will support the business drivers, business needs, and expected performance and close the performance gap? If the answer is yes, you can proceed to the next activity, identifying resources.

Worksheet 4.1: Aligning Specifications (Requested or Potential Solution: Training for Customer Information System Conversion)

1 Business Driver	2 Business Need	3 Expected Performance	4 Performance Gap and How Solution Will Close It	5 Specifications
Loss of market share (competition)	To support increased customer data needs and operational requirements. Customer sales have decreased because incorrect data has resulted in inaccurate orders and other problems.	To use the new customer information system to provide customers with excellent service and to increase sales.	The new CIS system would provide information to the salesforce regarding customers so that the right products can be matched to their needs.	The self-study module will be delivered via the Web within the system specifications for bandwidth, system performance time, and graphic ability (delivery methods and media, format and look). The solution will prepare the audience for the classroom training by • communicating the purpose of the training and expected results • presenting the functions of the new system and why the new system is being installed (outcomes and results).

If the answer is no, then you will have to determine where the process broke down and what you should do about it. Perhaps you have to go back to those who helped determine the specifications to clarify their thoughts, or you may need to go back to the analysis findings to make sure they were communicated correctly. In any event, you will need to back up, but probably not too far if you have followed all the steps in Rapid Needs Analysis process.

Identifying Resources

Now that you have validated the specifications, you will have enough information to identify the resources you will need to complete the development and implementation of the identified solution. You will then be able to determine the resources you have and what resources you will need to acquire.

To calculate the resources, it is important to know how much time it will take to develop the solution. The specifications should tell you the length of each component of the solution. Let's say, for example, that a computer-based training (CBT) self-study component will take four hours to complete. Now you need to translate this into development time. Table 4.6 lists the average development time for the most commonly used WLP media and methods.

The amount of resources required to develop the identified solution depends entirely on what the solution is, so forecasting resources is done on a case-by-case basis. You may find it helpful to consider the following when you begin this forecast:

- How complex is the content? The more complex, the more diverse the instructional design talent needed.

- How specialized is the content? More specialized content requires more subject matter expert time.

- How diverse is the audience? The more diverse, the more instructional design talent is needed.

- What media will be used to deliver the solution?
  - Classroom instruction probably needs only instructional designers and potentially graphics, layout, and production support.
  - Depending on what type of CBT is being developed, systems experts or instructional designers savvy in authoring tools and technology are required.

- Interactive instruction needs instructional designers who are expert in authoring tools and technology. Moreover, some (or a lot of) systems talent and designers with authoring tool, technology, and Web design talent in addition to graphics and layout talent most likely will be required.

- EPSS design requires design talent, systems talent, some layout talent, and often technical writing talent.

- Job aids usually require design talent and then, depending on the complexity of the tool, graphics support and possibly layout and production support.

- How much technological support is available (e.g., authoring tool availability), how new is the media, and what is the experience level with the media?

- How stable is the solution? The more unstable it is, the greater the impact will be on everyone's time.

Table 4.7 uses a grid to project the resources needed for the development and implementation of a solution. An example of resource projections for some human resources is provided. You can use the same grid to project resources needed for your solution. Review the resource categories listed in the first and second columns, and then identify the resources needed for your solution. Next, link those resources to key specifications to be sure you have the right resources. Finally, determine if these resources are available to you now or if you will need additional funding to obtain them.

Identifying Costs

Now that you know the resources that are required to develop and implement the solution, it is time to identify the costs of the solution in both hard and soft dollars. *Hard dollars* you will need to pay for directly out of pocket (such as purchasing new computers), and *soft dollars* are indirect costs, such as borrowing a programmer from another department, that the company would expend anyway, but perhaps in a different way. Worksheet 4.2 can help you list the cost categories that should relate to the resources you have identified in the previous section of the chapter.

Table 4.6: Development Time for WLP Methods and Media

Method or Media	Time Required to Develop	Resources Required
Classroom	30 to 45 hours of development per hour of instruction, depending on complexity of solution • Analysis (4–10 hours) • Design (3–9 hours) • Development (16–18 hours) • Review and revision (7–8 hours)	Instructional design talent Graphic layout talent
Computer-based training	50 to 150 hours of development per hour of instruction, depending on whether it is knowledge based, skill based, or attitude based and whether it is interactive and to what extent • Analysis (5–25 hours) • Design (15–50 hours) • Development (25–60 hours) • Review and revision (5–15 hours)	Instructional design talent Authoring tool or systems talent Graphic layout talent Production talent
Interactive multimedia	100 to 250 hours of development per hour of instruction (potentially less depending on the authoring tool used and the experience of the developers and programmers) • Analysis (15–30 hours) • Design (25–50 hours) • Development (45–125 hours) • Review and revision (15–35 hours)	Instructional design talent Authoring tool or systems talent Graphic layout talent
Electronic performance support system	100 to 250 hours of development per hour of instruction (potentially less depending on the authoring tool used and the experience of the developers and programmers) • Analysis (15–30 hours) • Design (25–50 hours) • Development (45–135 hours) • Review and revision (15–35 hours)	Instructional design talent Authoring tool or systems talent Technical writing talent Graphic layout talent
Job aid	50 to 75 hours of development time depending on the media of the job aid, the structure, and the complexity • Analysis (8–10 hours) • Design (15–25 hours) • Development (20–30 hours) • Review and revision (7–10 hours)	Instructional design talent Graphic layout talent Production talent

Table 4.7: Resource Projection Worksheet

Type of Resource	Specific Resource Required	How Linked to Specifications	Have or Can Borrow	Need
Human resources	Material developers (e.g., designers, developers, programmers)	Two designers needed for computer-based training (CBT)	1 full-time equivalent (FTE)/0.5 FTE	0.5 FTE
		Two programmers needed for CBT	0 FTE	2 FTE
		One developer needed for classroom training	1 FTE	0 FTE
	Trainers (in-house, full-time, part-time, external)	Four trainers needed to provide train-the-trainer for classroom training	3 FTE/1 FTE	0 FTE
		12 trainers needed in regions to provide classroom training	4 FTE/6 FTE	2 FTE
	Material reviewers and revisers (subject matter experts, managers, participants)			
	Administrative support			
	Subject matter experts			
Technology	Software (visual basic, authoring tool, graphics capability, networking needs, bandwidth considerations)			
Equipment	Hardware (e.g., computers, computer projectors, satellite dishes)			
Facilities	Rooms (available or need to rent)			

Identifying Risks Versus Benefits

Once you know the resources and costs for the solution, you should have enough information to identify the risks associated with it. Identifying potential risks will help you prepare for gaining approval from the solution's sponsor to move forward with development. You should weigh the risks against the benefits of the solution for the organization in closing the performance gap. At this point the benefits had better outweigh the risks, or you'll have a big problem on your hands. There should be no problem, however, given all

Worksheet 4.2: Cost Identification

Cost Categories	Hard Dollars	Soft Dollars
Project management		
• Salaries		
• Travel and living expenses		
• Lost opportunity		
Material development (including developer and programmer costs)		
• Paper based		
• Video		
• Audio		
• Computer- or Web-based training		
Material review and revision		
• Material review		
• Material revision (pre and post pilot)		
Trainers		
• Salaries		
• Travel and living expenses		
Participants		
• Salaries		
• Travel and living expenses		
• Lost opportunity		
Materials		
• CD-ROMs		
• Paper materials		
Equipment		
• Video players		
• Video and CD-ROM reproduction equipment		
• Computers		
Facilities		
• Rented or allocated use of classrooms		
• Lunches and refreshments		

Worksheet 4.2: Cost Identification (continued)

Cost Categories	Hard Dollars	Soft Dollars
Administrative support		
• Copying materials and disks		
• Registration		
• Record keeping and reporting		
• Distribution		
Subject matter experts		
• Salaries		
• Travel and living expenses		
Pilot costs		
• Facilities		
• Facilitators		
• Materials		
• Coordination		
Evaluation strategy		
• Salaries		
• Tool development		
• Systems for analysis and reporting		
Incentives and recognition		
• Financial incentives		
• Rewards (plaques, gift certificates)		
Supporting materials		
• Graphics		
• Clip art packages		
Installation		
• Equipment		
• Software		

---

of the checkpoints and validations you have completed throughout the process.

You can use worksheet 4.3 to identify the risks of moving forward with the development of the identified solution. Questions to help you identify the risks most often associated with developing a solution are listed in the first column. Review these questions, and place a checkmark in either the yes or no column to indicate if a risk exists. When you have completed this worksheet, you should have a feel for where the weaknesses of the project are and whether the risk involved in developing the solution outweighs the benefit of the solution.

When you have completed the risk identification and determined that the benefit does outweigh the risk, you have all of the information needed to move

Worksheet 4.3: Solution Risk Identification Worksheet

Potential Risk	Yes	No
Is the company reorganizing?	❏	❏
Is the timing right, given the political environment?	❏	❏
Do key stakeholders support the solution?	❏	❏
Is there a budget for the solution?	❏	❏
Is the content for the solution stable?	❏	❏
Are the systems and processes that will support the solution stable?	❏	❏
Are the required resources available?	❏	❏
Is the technology available to support the solution?	❏	❏
Is the target audience motivated to participate in the solution?	❏	❏
Identify other risks here:	❏	❏

on to the final activity in step 4, which is to gain the sponsor's approval to develop the solution.

Gaining Approval

The last activity in step 4 is to gain approval from the sponsor who will authorize the budget and allocate resources for the development and implementation of the solution. You should meet with the person or people and walk through your key findings, asking at the conclusion for approval. Review the following with the sponsor before asking for approval:

- how the solution (based on the specifications) aligns with the business drivers, business needs, expected performance outcomes, and performance gap and how it will close the gap

- the definition of the solution (e.g., CBT, classroom training, EPSS, job aid)

- the resources needed and the cost of the resources

- the benefits of the costs and the risk involved in not developing the solution.

If you do not gain approval at this point, it probably is not due to anything you or those involved in the analysis have done. Lack of approval most often is based on an organizational change that is out of your control (and probably that of the sponsor). Chances are that you will gain approval and will be ready to move on to step 5, which involves gaining the commitment of everyone who will be involved in the solution.

Chapter Summary

The main focus of this chapter was on determining the specifications for the identified solution by quickly applying the analysis findings to speed up the design and development. Solution specifications were defined and case examples of how they were determined presented. Identifying who should be involved in the determination was discussed, as well as how to communicate the purpose of the determination and specific roles and responsibilities. How and why to discuss the data analysis findings and how to translate them to specifications were introduced. The different methods for determining specifications were provided, along with how to validate the resulting specifications. Identifying resources and calculating costs were introduced, and how to calculate the risks involved in moving forward with the design and development was addressed. Finally, how to gain sponsor approval was discussed.

Discussion Questions

The following questions are provided to help you apply what you learned in this chapter:

- What are solution specifications, and why is determining them important before engaging in design and development?

  _____

  _____

- Thinking of a current analysis project, who within your organization would be best able to determine solution specifications? Why?

  _____

  _____

- What is important to communicate to those involved regarding the purpose, roles, and responsibility involved in determining specifics?

  _____

  _____

- Why is it important to discuss the findings of the needs analysis with those involved in determining specifications?

  _____

  _____

- What method of specification determination would work best in your organization? Why?

  _____

  _____

- Why is validating the specifications with the requester and the target audience important?

  _____

  _____

- How does knowing the time it will take to develop a solution assist in calculating resources?

  _____

  _____

- How is resource identification linked to cost identification?

  _____

  _____

- What is the purpose of calculating the risks involved in moving forward with designing and developing the identified solution based on the final specifications?

  _____

  _____

- What should you do if you do not gain approval for the solution?

  _____

  _____

5

Step 5: Gaining Commitment

At this point in the Rapid Needs Analysis process you have approval to move forward with developing the solution and are ready to gain commitment from those who will be involved in designing, developing, and using the solution. *Gaining commitment* means communicating the need for and benefits of the solution, or "selling" the solution, to ensure the agreement and cooperation of those you will depend on to make it work.

There is no scientific method for gaining commitment, but the key components for success include the following:

- Build relationships with stakeholders, solution developers, subject matter experts, the target audience and their managers, and supervisors so that you and the solution are perceived as credible.

- Provide the information needed by each person or group involved so they can make an informed commitment.

- Recognize and address needs, objections, and concerns early in the process to prevent resistance and problems from surfacing later on.

At the end of step 5 you will know

- if you have the commitment of the designers and developers or others required to develop the solution.

Case Examples

Gaining commitment from those who will develop and implement the solution is critical to getting to the right solution. The following case examples illustrate how two different organizations gained commitment for their solutions.

Case Example 1

A manufacturer of computer hardware approved the development of an intensive five-day classroom training for its sales professionals, who were selling multi-million-dollar products to customers worldwide. The purpose of the training was to increase product knowledge and competitor knowledge and to introduce and develop a new sales process. The training needed to be designed, developed, and piloted within two months.

Although the training was seen as important and the sales management team and other stakeholders desired classroom training, there was considerable resistance among the solution developers to this method of training. They believed that a combination of Web-based training for product knowledge and classroom training for the sales process would be more cost-effective and build skills more quickly. Because the success of the solution depended heavily on the involvement and cooperation of the developers, the solution project manager had to actively sell the benefits of this method.

Through group and individual meetings the project manager determined that the major point of resistance was the fact that lots of money was being pumped into the program and that, in the long run, offering only classroom training would become very expensive. In addition, the developers felt that classroom method was antiquated and that as part of the technology industry, they should be offering more leading-edge training methods.

It was difficult to overcome this resistance; although Web-based training could not be developed in two months, it was a much longer term solution. What the project manager did was to clearly point out the benefits of the program and the income the company would realize if the program were a success in the short term. She also focused on how the success of the program would build the developers' credibility and visibility within the organization and demonstrate their ability to be flexible in responding to training needs by putting the business first. She also explained that in designing the classroom materials they could begin to position (with their stakeholders) how the same materials could be used to produce Web-based materials for long-term use.

As a way to recognize the issue, the project manager worked with the developers to build a case for the long-term benefits of converting the original classroom materials into Web-based materials. The classroom was billed as a less expensive way to test the materials and prototype the content for the long-term solution than developing the Web-based training.

The classroom training turned out to be a tremendous success because, even though it was developed quickly, it was sound. As a result, the company's income and profits increased substantially. Through this success, management agreed that the classroom would become part of the overall curriculum and that it would be converted to just-in-time Web-based offerings.

Case Example 2

The field area manager of a national auto insurance company came to the WLP manager and requested a curriculum that would support the nuts and bolts of the company's sales and service activities in the field offices. The specification determination team identified eight modules that would be part of a self-study Web-based training program. Included was a module on claims and adjustments.

Although the manager of claims and adjustments had been part of the specification determination, he did not think the field should be trained in claims and adjustments. He believed that all inquires should be dealt with by his central department and that the field staff should immediately refer any questions to the department. Although the content in the module was informational and would allow the field to handle only basic inquires during the sales and service process, he was adamant that claims information was much too sophisticated for the field.

The field area manager, on the other hand, was delighted with the recommended eight modules (including the information provided in claims and adjustments). She said the curriculum was up to date and matched the results of the customer surveys about how field staff could better support their inquiries.

The WLP manager had to sell the training course to the claims and adjustments manager to gain his commitment to provide the subject matter expertise needed. The WLP manager met with the field area manager and explained the claims and adjustments manager's concerns regarding the inclusion of the claims and adjustment information. Together they discussed the business and customer benefits and developed a presentation they would make together to the claims and adjustments manager.

During the meeting the field manager explained the problems she was seeing in the field and presented the customer survey data that showed growing dissatisfaction with the field. A competitive research best practices study was completed as part of the needs analysis, and the results indicated that all of the company's key competitors provided basic claims and adjustment information in the field. The WLP manager acknowledged the claims and adjustments manager's concerns and asked how he thought WLP could ensure compliance with insurance regulations but also meet customer demand and stay competitive. The three managers worked together to build an outline for a job aid. This aid would be used to answer basic claims and adjust-

ment questions and provide a process for referring customers to the claims and adjustments department for more sensitive matters in a way that was customer friendly and advantageous to both the customer and the company.

Step 5 Activities

You will complete two activities in step 5 of the Rapid Needs Analysis process:

1. identifying who needs to commit to the solution and why

2. selling the benefits of their involvement.

Identifying Those Who Need to Commit

The first activity in step 5 is identifying who needs to commit to the solution and why. Knowing this will help you customize your "sale" and garner the support you will need for the solution. Table 5.1 is a tool you can use to help identify those who will need to commit to the solution. The people or groups most frequently involved are listed in column 1, and the reasons why you need their commitment are listed in column 2.

It is likely that most of the people identified in table 5.1 were involved in determining the specifications for the solution, so they already will have some background information about the solution. This experience should have provided them with a firm understanding of the solution's purpose and expected results and should enable them to make a commitment more quickly.

Selling the Benefits

Once you have identified who will be involved in the solution, their roles, and why they need to commit, your job is to ask for the commitment and "close the sale." Sometimes your pitch is made in a meeting that includes everyone, and sometimes it is made in smaller group meetings determined by the participant's role in the solution. The decision about whom to involve in what meetings is largely determined by the location and availability of those whose attendance is required.

Usually commitment meetings are held in person because it is easier to influence others and sell ideas face to face. However, if in-person meetings are not practical, then conference calls or Webcasts can work if the information you will review is available electronically during or before the meeting.

Once you have worked out the logistics of these meetings, it is time to plan for the content of the meeting and how you will go about gaining commitment.

Table 5.1: Who Needs to Commit?

Who Needs to Commit	Why They Need to Commit
Stakeholders	It is essential that stakeholders who were not part of the approval process agree with the solution and commit to supporting its development and implementation. They are the critical link between the business and the solution.
Subject matter experts	Because of their knowledge and expertise, the commitment of subject matter experts is critical to the success of the solution. As with the developers, if these experts are not committed to providing the required content, the solution will not succeed.
Solution developers	Solution developers will design and develop the solution, and their understanding and support of the solution are imperative. If they are not committed to developing the best solution possible, the solution will not succeed. If external developers will be used, this is the time to procure them and gain their commitment.
Managers and supervisors of participants	Managers and supervisors of the participants may be subject matter experts. They also will support the solution in the field and need to understand its importance and their role in its success. They are the link to the audience and must commit to communicating its benefits to the audience and, in many cases, coaching employees once they complete the solution.
Participants	Most often solution participants are not asked to make a commitment to the solution until the solution is piloted, unless they will be involved as subject matter experts or as "reality orienters." It is wise, however, to plan ahead for how you will gain commitment from pilot participants and participants overall. They are the ones who ultimately will take part in the solution and will transfer the knowledge, skills, processes, and tools to their work.

Gaining commitment in this context usually involves the following steps:

First, communicate the background of the solution and answer any questions. If the people involved in the commitment meetings have not been involved in specification determination or informational meetings, or if considerable time has elapsed, it is important to communicate the following:

- key findings of the needs analysis
- specifications related to the analysis conclusions and recommendations
- how the organization will benefit from the solution.

This information will provide a frame of reference for their role in developing the solution.

Second, communicate each person's role in developing the solution, including why they were chosen and what they are expected to do, and answer any questions about roles.

Next, communicate the benefits of committing to the solution and answer any questions. You should discuss the following topics:

- What's in it for the stakeholders, subject matter experts, solution developers, managers and supervisors, and participants to commit to the solution?
- How will the results of the commitment pay off?
- What are the risks of not implementing the solution?
- How will the benefits be monitored so those involved can see the payoff of their commitment as the project evolves?

Potential benefits of committing to developing the solution are listed in table 5.2.

Finally, overcome concerns and resistance to committing to the solution in the following ways:

- Identify potential resistance as soon as possible, and discuss concerns.
- Probe for more information and potential hidden agendas.
- Determine if the objection is "real" or if it is a diversion from the real objection.

Table 5.2: Why Commit?

Who Needs to Commit	Benefits of Committing
Stakeholders	If the solution meets the business need and closes the performance gap, they will succeed in their jobs. Their credibility will increase because they were involved in a successful solution.
Subject matter experts	They will gain recognition for their knowledge and expertise. Their credibility and stature in the company will increase because of their role in developing the solution. They will contribute to closing the performance gap and meeting the business need.
Solution developers	They will gain recognition for their knowledge and expertise. Their credibility and stature in the company will increase because of their role in developing the solution. They will contribute to closing the performance gap and meeting the business need.
Managers and supervisors of participants	If subject matter experts, they will gain recognition for their knowledge and expertise. Their involvement and commitment to the solution will show in the end results of the solution. They will contribute to closing the performance gap and meeting the business need.
Participants	If subject matter experts, they will gain recognition for their knowledge and expertise. If involved in the pilot, they will provide information that will make the solution stronger and more successful. If participants only, their use of the solution's knowledge, skills, processes, or tools will lead to the organization's (as well as their personal) success.

- Deal with objections and resistance fairly but firmly. Be clear about what will and will not happen and why.

- Negotiate, when and if negotiation is possible. Some activities or tasks may be negotiable as long as any changes do not compromise the integrity of the solution.

Resistance or disagreement often is a result of not knowing or misunderstanding the customer or business need. By using the information gathered during the analysis to link the solution to the business, you will be able to overcome resistance from those needed to build the solution. Presenting this information and then asking for their assistance in ensuring that the solution meets the identified needs and the expected outcomes will enable you to counteract resistance to the recommended solution. Worksheet 5.1 provides a set of questions to prepare you to present your case to those resisting the approved solution.

Keep in mind that gaining commitment is not a one-time task, but needs to be revisited frequently throughout the life of the project. If you continue with the development of the solution in a project management role, then you should plan for regaining commitment from those involved at regular intervals. If you hand the project off at the end of the analysis, you should communicate the need for periodically regaining commitment with the parties responsible for the development.

Worksheet 5.1 Selling Customer and Business Benefits to Resisters

Questions	Your Case
What key business drivers will this solution support? How does the resistance affect these drivers?	
What business and customer information collected during the analysis provides factual support for the solution?	
If the resistance is not overcome, how will the business and customer be affected?	
How will the resister's participation benefit the business or customer?	
Who else can assist in presenting the business and customer case, and how?	
What concerns does the resister have, and how should they be integrated into the solution to better support the customer and business?	
What other business and customer information would be helpful in selling the approved solution to the resister?	
What would be the outcome of the resister's not participating in the solution?	

Chapter Summary

This chapter provided information about how to gain commitment from those who will develop and implement the identified solution. Two major activities were addressed in this chapter: 1) how to identify who needs to commit to the solution and why, and 2) how to sell the benefits of involvement in developing the solution. Case examples were provided that illustrated how two very different companies approached gaining commitment, and three tools were provided to assist in this step in the process.

Discussion Questions

The following questions are provided to help you apply what you learned in this chapter:

- Why is gaining commitment important in moving forward with the development and eventual implementation of the solution?

- Who typically needs to commit to the solution's development and implementation?

  _____

  _____

- Why are these people important to the solution's success?

  _____

  _____

- Why is gaining commitment similar to closing a sale?

  _____

  _____

- What are some ways to gain commitment?

  _____

  _____

- How does focusing on customer and business needs help gain commitment to the solution?

  _____

  _____

- What are some of the benefits that could be realized by those who will need to commit?

  _____

  _____

6

Step 6: Initiating Development of the Solution

Now that you have the commitment of all who will be involved in the development and implementation of the solution, the official handoff from the analysis phase to the development phase takes place. This handoff involves working with the solution developers to create a design document for the solution and completing a development project plan. This collaboration will ensure that the analysis findings and related specifications will be correctly translated into the final design for the course and that the developers have a plan to manage their development activities.

At this point you should be clear about the following:

- the business purpose of the solution
- the performance need the solution will address
- the definition of the solution (e.g., computer-based training, a workshop, a job aid, classroom training, a combination)
- the team you will work with to design and develop the solution.

When the design document is completed, reviewed, and approved, responsibility for solution development is transferred to the development team.

At the end of this step you will

- have a detailed blueprint for how the solution will be developed
- have a project plan for the development phase
- conclude the analysis phase of the WLP process.

Case Examples

Initiating the development of the solution can happen differently in different situations. The following case examples describe how two companies approached this step of the Rapid Needs Analysis very differently but with positive results.

Case Example 1

The engineers in a division of a high-tech manufacturing company who 15 years ago invented state-of-the-art technology were beginning to retire. The organization was concerned that the bulk of its brainpower would soon be walking out the door and wanted to transfer this knowledge to engineers with less experience and expertise. The WLP manager was involved in conducting a needs analysis to quickly determine what the engineers at lower levels needed to know to become masters and how to transfer this knowledge. This need was urgent because once the masters left the company, so did its greatest competitive advantage.

The identified solution was a competency identification program and fast-track training curriculum that would be customized to each engineer's competency levels and knowledge and skill needs. The master engineers would play a big part in transferring their knowledge to the other engineers.

A representative group of the master engineers was involved in providing information throughout the 10-day analysis, including determining the specifications, so it made perfect sense for them to help create the design documents. Because the solution was critical and the need to develop it urgent, the sponsor (who was also the requester) took part in the specifications determination meeting and approved the results on the spot. This paved the way for the WLP manager, sponsor, and requester to gain commitment from everyone involved and to initiate the development of the solution.

It took 1.5 days to create the design document for a very complex solution. Besides the master engineers and the sponsor, the WLP manager and two solution designers were involved. Once the design documents were completed, the WLP manager created the project plan and distributed it to everyone involved. Because all of the key players and decision makers were involved in the majority of the analysis, transfer to the development team was seamless.

Case Example 2

A high-end catalog retailer was experiencing trouble with its telephone call centers. Customer and employee complaints had been increasing steadily over six months. The major customer complaints were receiving conflicting information about order status and shipping dates and being told, "I can't help you, the computers are down." The major employee complaint was having stale or inaccurate information on their computer systems and having to deal with irate customers. Members of the call center WLP team conducted a needs analysis to determine what the problem was and how it could be fixed.

The identified solution was an electronic performance support system (EPSS) that would provide up-to-the-minute information on products, shipping, customer accounts, and sales and service processes. The solution would involve not only a new system, but training in how to use it.

Once they received the specifications and the WLP manager gained commitment to develop the solution, the solution development team created the design documents. These documents were completed in one week and were reviewed by programmers, key stakeholders, subject matter experts, and sample groups of audience supervisors and audience members. The reviewers were briefed on their review role and responsibility and received the design documents by email prior to the review meeting. The meeting took place via Webcast so that those in call centers in outlying regions also could take part in the discussion. When the documents were stable, the WLP manager asked for and gained approval from the requester (the general manager of call center operations) to begin developing the solution.

After the WLP manager and the lead solution developer completed the development project plan, the responsibility for developing the solution was officially handed off to the lead developer.

Step 6 Activities

Three activities are completed in step 6:

1. creating a design document for the solution
2. creating a development project plan
3. transferring responsibility for the development of the solution to the development team.

Creating a Design Document for the Solution

A design document is a road map or a blueprint for how the solution will be developed, what it will (and will not) contain, how results will be measured, and how and what needs the solution addresses. Creating design documents is frequently skipped, but often with disastrous results. Design and development can be costly propositions. If the design is faulty and does

not properly represent the specifications identified in step 4, the resulting solution might miss the business and performance mark. If this happens, then re-work and additional resources may be required, meaning even more time and money spent on the solution. Loss of credibility for those involved in the analysis, design, development, and implementation is another costly result of faulty design.

In the past, the creation of design documents has been one of the first activities in the solution development phase. Moving it to the end of the analysis phase ensures a better linkage to the specifications, the analysis findings, and the business and performance needs. A tighter information loop exists when the analysis and design are completed in the same cycle and analysis participants take part in engineering the design.

Design Document Content

A design document usually contains the following information:

- the performance need (based on knowledge and skill requirements), expressed as "performance objectives"
- the specific content of the solution
- the references or resources for the creation of the solution (including the content resources or references, such as a policy guide or another training course or process)
- the evaluation method for determining if the solution adequately addresses the performance need and consequent business need (e.g., test, observation, skill practice)
- the existing materials that support the solution
- the pre and post work, if any, or the prerequisites
- the estimated length of the solution or a particular component of the solution.

Tool 6.1 is an example of a design document format that has been used successfully to design numerous solutions, both paper and computer based. All of the information listed above is reflected in this document. The example described in the design document is the development of classroom training for a technical sales team.

Performance Objectives

The knowledge and skills required for the solution, identified in the specifications determined in step 4,

Tool 6.1: Design Document Format

Delivery method: Classroom
Module: Overview
Estimated length: 60 minutes

Prerequisite: Products and Competitor Products CBT
Post work: None

Knowledge or Skill Gap	Performance Objective	Content	Resources	Evaluation	Supporting Materials
Product or service knowledge	Using the job aids, the participant will be able to describe the organization's vision in his or her own words.	The organization's structure Specific information on global operations Specific information on regional salesforces The vision The services	Organization chart Vision statement Descriptions of each regional salesforce Regional organization charts Descriptions of services	Self-efficacy rating on readiness to implement the vision	Job aids Organization charts Key players and contact information Vision statement

are extremely important in identifying the performance objectives for the solution. Performance objectives are used to link the solution back to the business and to describe what the target audience will know and be able to do as a result of the solution. These objectives are seen as the backbone of the design for your solution. Once developed, you will be able to use the objectives to measure if the solution is on target.

Performance objectives should describe the following elements:

- the task that must be improved through the solution

- how the task is to be performed following the solution

- what performance indicator will measure how well or to what extent the employee performs the task following a successful solution.

An example of a performance objective for time management is, "At the completion of the Time Management workshop, the associate will use the Franklin Prioritization Tool to organize the critical tasks to complete the Funds Management Report for the day by the 3 p.m. cutoff time."

You can use worksheet 6.1 in developing performance objectives. In the right-hand column, list the objective corresponding to the performance objective

components in the first column. The middle column was completed using the time management performance objective example.

Team Review and Approval

Review and approval of the design documents is a necessary task but one that can be completed quickly. Usually a review team that will be involved throughout the design and development of the solution is identified at this point. Most often this team consists of representatives from the following groups: key stakeholders, subject matter experts, audience managers and supervisors, audience members, and solution designers.

Key stakeholders, including the requester, will make sure the design meets the business and performance needs and will validate that the performance objectives are realistic and will build the required knowledge and skills. If the sponsor is the WLP manager, this person will also be involved in the review.

Subject matter experts will validate that the content identified is correct and stable (e.g., validate that a process has not changed between analysis and design). Subject matter experts may be able to identify where resources for developing the course can be found.

Audience managers and supervisors will ensure that the design will build the required knowledge and

---

Worksheet 6.1: Performance Objective Diagram

Performance Objective Component	Example Objective	Your Objective
The task to be performed	Complete the Funds Management Report	
How the task is to be performed	Use the Franklin Prioritization Tool to organize the critical tasks	
How well the individual must perform the task or to what extent	For the day by the 3 p.m. cut-off time	

skills and will assess whether it will produce a realistic solution that will meet the identified business need. They should be able to flag where the design will not work in the environment. Managers and supervisors may be able to identify where resources for developing the course can be found.

Much like managers and supervisors, audience members will make sure the design will build the required knowledge and skills and produce a realistic solution. They too should be able to flag where the design will not work in the environment and may be good sources for finding course development resources. This group sees the design from the user point of view.

Solution designers who were not involved in developing the design documents will provide a quality control check on the design itself.

The following six activities will help you complete the design document review:

1. Set a meeting time to review the design documents. This meeting can take place in person or be conducted via Webcast or conference call. The meeting may last two to three hours, depending on the length of the solution or solution component.

2. Send the design documents to the review team at least 24 hours before the review meeting.

3. Set an agenda for the meeting, and communicate what you want specific members of the review team to look for.

4. Set ground rules for how the review will be conducted, and explain the difference between reviewing and approving the design documents.

5. Walk through the document objective by objective and discuss the related content, resources, evaluation, and supporting materials.

6. Modify or change the design documents based on group consensus.

Requester Approval and Sign-off

The requester of the solution usually approves the design documents and signs off on them. This person has been close to the needs analysis throughout the process and should understand the link between the design and solving the performance and business need. Additionally, this person usually has the authority to sign off on this critical piece of the analysis.

Creating a Development Project Plan

A project plan is needed to communicate development responsibilities, time lines, and deliverables. Planning is always important, but it is even more so when solutions need to be developed quickly. Collaborating with the solution developers to create this plan will ensure that they have a thorough understanding of the development process and maintain their commitment to it.

At this point in the Rapid Needs Analysis process you have identified the performance gap, determined and gained approval for the specifications for the solution, linked the specifications to the solution's development through the design document, and gained final approval for the overall design document. The work that remains is the development of the solution. One of the final activities in the Rapid Needs Analysis process is to kick off the development through documenting a project plan.

A development project plan template is provided in tool 6.2. The template lists the major milestones and deliverables that are part of Rapid Solution Development. You can enter the content of this plan into your project planning program to expedite the planning process. Timelines for completing the milestones are dependent on the type of solution being developed and, therefore, are not included in this prototype.

Tool 6.2: Prototype of a Rapid Solution Development Project Plan

Step 1: Identifying the Evaluation Approach

Major Milestones

- Determine how the solution's effectiveness will be linked to the performance gap and business drivers.
- Identify how the solution's effectiveness will be evaluated.
- Develop the instruments needed to conduct the evaluation.
- Determine who needs to be involved in the evaluation and their roles and responsibilities.
- Communicate the evaluation approach to appropriate parties.

Deliverables

- Evaluation plan
- Evaluation instruments
- Evaluation communication document

Step 2: Developing Draft Materials or Storyboards

Major Milestones

- Sequence the performance objectives.
- Identify learning or performance activities.
- Create materials or storyboards as designed.

Deliverables

- Material or storyboard drafts

Step 3: Establishing the Review Process

Major Milestones

- Identify reviewers and establish roles and responsibilities. (This team most likely has been selected to review the design documents.)
- Identify a standardized communication process.
- Establish a review process and guidelines.
- Conduct a review kickoff meeting.

Deliverables

- Review of process and guidelines
- Report of kickoff meeting

Step 4: Conducting the Review

Major Milestones

- Consolidate review findings.
- Negotiate and prioritize changes.
- Document results.
- Communicate results.

Deliverables

- Review results document

(continued on next page)

Tool 6.2: Prototype of a Rapid Solution Development Project Plan (continued)

Step 5: Finalize the Drafts or Storyboards

Major Milestones

- Integrate findings into drafts or storyboards.
- Present final version to approvers.
- Test process for production or system upload.
- Obtain sign-off on final materials or storyboards.

Deliverables

- Final version of materials or storyboards
- Process for production or system upload implemented for pilot
- Sign-off on final version

Step 6: Piloting the Solution

Major Milestones

- Develop a pilot plan.
- Develop the tools needed to implement the pilot.
- Communicate roles and responsibilities to pilot audience.
- Conduct the pilot.
- Evaluate the results and recommend any necessary changes.
- Communicate the results and recommendations.
- Obtain sign-off to make recommended changes (if needed).
- Make recommended changes (if needed).

Deliverables

- Solution pilot
- Recommendations for changes (if needed)
- Final version of solution

Step 7: Implementing the Solution

Major Milestones

- Hand off the final version of the solution to those who will implement.
- Finalize the process for material production and distribution or system upload.

Deliverables

- Final version of solution
- Final process for distribution

Transferring Responsibility for Solution Development

When the design document and development project plan have been completed, the official handoff from design to development takes place. A formal transfer meeting between the analysis and development project mangers is highly recommended so that nothing falls through the cracks and the design can proceed smoothly to development.

Chapter Summary

The focus of this last chapter of *Rapid Needs Analysis* was on initiating the development of the solution through the creation of design documents and a development project plan. Completing these two activities marks the final transition between the analysis and development phases. Case examples were provided that described how two different companies initiated the development phase and transferred responsibility for the solution to the developers.

Discussion Questions

The following questions are provided to help you apply what you learned in this chapter:

- What is a design document, and why is it important at this point in the analysis process?

- What are the elements of a design document?

- Why is identifying performance objectives an important part of creating design documents?

- Who should be involved in reviewing the design documents, and why?

- What activities are involved in reviewing design documents?

- What is the purpose of creating a development project plan at this point in the analysis?

Appendix A:
Index of Tables, Worksheets, Tools, and Figures

Chapter 3

Chapter 4

Chapter 5

Chapter 6

Appendix B: Glossary

best practices literature search—A data collection method to determine how other organizations with similar performance problems or needs have solved their problems and to identify industry trends.

business drivers—The internal and external factors that drive an organization's strategy and therefore its business and performance needs. An example of an external business driver is government; regulation or deregulation forces changes in competition or the overall business environment. An example of an internal business driver is technology; new innovations in technology create opportunities or needs for changes in information storage and processing.

business need—A requirement identified by an organization through examining business drivers and determining how the company needs to respond to an external or internal force. Examples of business needs include to increase competitive advantage, to increase sales, and to develop new products more quickly.

content analysis—A method of examining qualitative data in a systematic, objective, and quantitative manner that involves the analysis and classification of data into major content areas.

customer and business benefits—What the organization and its customers will gain as a result of the solution.

customers—The individuals who use WLP products and services. Some are paying customers, who may be the same as or different from those who participate; others may depend on the results of the products or services to meet specific business outcomes.

data analysis—Examination of the information collected during the needs analysis to determine what it means.

data bias—Prejudice or corruption of the data that leads to flawed data analysis. For example, if the data analyst has strong beliefs about the intervention being evaluated, these beliefs could influence the way the analysis is conducted and contaminate the data.

data comparison—Comparison of raw data to condensed data to ensure that the data has not been distorted. Data comparison is aided by chronological arrangement, partition, cause and effect, or classification.

data collection instrument—A tool used to collect the data needed for Rapid Needs Analysis, such as a survey, observation worksheet, or focus group interview guide.

data collection method—Means of collecting information during a Rapid Needs Analysis. Data collection methods include online surveys, electronic focus groups, best practices literature searches, job mapping, observations, and telephone interviews.

data interpretation—Translation of data results into conclusions and recommendations.

design document—A road map or a blueprint for how the solution will be developed, what it will (and will not) contain, how results will be measured, and how and what needs the solution addresses.

development project plan—A document used to communicate the responsibilities, time lines, and deliverables for a solution development project.

electronic performance support system (EPSS)—A computer-based system used to provide job-related information to employees as they do their jobs.

expected outcomes—What the requester wants the audience to do as a result of the solution, such as sell more products, reduce scrap, decrease design time, or decrease the time to market.

focus group—A data collection method consisting of a structured meeting using a predeveloped script to obtain specific information. Focus groups usually are conducted in person, but sometimes they are conducted using Web technology like interactive chat rooms or satellite technology.

handoff from analysis to development—The official transfer of responsibility for the solution from the needs analysis project manager to the development project manager.

identifying costs—The process of determining the financial costs of developing the solution.

identifying the current situation—Quickly gathering information about what is happening within the organization, how the target audience is performing currently, what environmental barriers need to be overcome, and the causes of performance problems.

intervention—A specific event or system that is implemented to close a performance gap.

interview guide—The questions and process used to conduct focus groups and telephone and in-person interviews.

job aid—A paper-based or online tool used to help employees improve the performance of a specific task. An example is a flowchart for a specific sales process.

job mapping—A data collection method consisting of a thorough walk-through of what individuals do in their jobs. Its purpose is to identify required job knowledge, skills, expected performance results, and barriers to doing the job.

needs analysis project plan—A document used to communicate the responsibilities, time lines, and deliverables for a needs analysis project.

observation—A data collection method that involves watching employees in their work environment perform tasks, use processes, and deliver services and products to determine skill and knowledge gaps as well as environmental flaws.

off-the-shelf data analysis tools—Instruments and programs for data analysis that are available for purchase.

online survey—An instrument used to collect data from the target audience during a Rapid Needs Analysis. Online surveys are much like paper-based surveys, except they are distributed and collected through a Website or via email.

performance gap—The difference between the expected or required performance or outcomes and the current performance as identified through the data analysis.

performance indicator—Variable that enables you to predict performance change so you can determine if an intervention will be successful.

performance measures—Units that gauge progress or change against an established standard that will be used to evaluate the solution's success.

performance need—How and to what extent performance must change to meet business needs and business drivers.

performance objectives—Descriptions of what the target audience will know and be able to do as a result of the solution that link the solution back to the business. Objectives are the backbone of the design and are used to measure if the solution is on target.

performance problem—Job performance that is not meeting expected outcomes or producing expected results.

process analysis—A method of examining process data that identifies the components or steps of a work process.

quantitative analysis—Scientific and statistical examination of quantitative data. Most often a computer is used to support the analysis.

Rapid Needs Analysis—A quick and efficient study that identifies a performance gap and determines a solution based on business and performance needs.

Rapid Needs Analysis process—The steps, methods, and tools that will quickly and efficiently identify a performance gap and determine a solution based on business and performance needs.

requester—The person who originally requested the needs analysis or a specific solution.

request parameters—The information provided to the requester early in the process to set clear expectations for a Rapid Needs Analysis.

resource identification—The process of determining what and who is needed to develop the identified solution.

sample selection procedures—Steps to take to ensure that the sample size is large enough to get a return rate that is scientifically adequate.

sample size—The number of sample members needed to ensure the data confidence level.

sampling frame—A representative sample, chosen through systematic (e.g., choosing one name from every 2,500) and simple (e.g., giving all names a number and choosing numbers from that list randomly) random sampling.

selling the benefits—Pointing out what those involved in the solution, the company, and its customers will gain from the solution.

solution—A system or method to resolve a performance problem. A solution typically is a combination of methods, such as training, incentives, or process improvements. A solution encompasses an intervention.

solution designers—The team responsible for designing and developing the solution based on the identified specifications. This team may consist of internal as well as external resources, including systems employees (if needed), designers, and writers.

solution risks—The weaknesses or potential vulnerabilities involved in developing the identified solution.

solution specifications—A detailed description of what will make the solution successful in meeting business needs, meeting performance needs, and closing the performance gap.

specification board—A forum, most often used in war rooms, for documenting suggestions and comments to inform the specifications for a solution. These boards can be physical or virtual, and there is one for each conclusion and supporting recommendation.

sponsor—The executive or manager who is supporting the needs analysis, who provides financial approval for it, and who navigates the political waters on its behalf.

stakeholders—The people who have the most to gain from the business outcome of the performance improvement the solution will provide. The key responsibility of the stakeholders is to ensure that the solution links to the business need.

subject matter experts—The people responsible for providing content information, including processes, procedures, and environmental data, so that the specifications result in a solution that will close the performance gap.

target audience—The employees who will take part in the identified solution.

telephone interviews—The use of predetermined questions in a one-to-one telephone conference to collect data from a specific audience.

validation—Confirmation or corroboration of a data component such as a performance need or the identified solution.

war room—A place where the details needed to design and develop a solution are planned without facilitation using specification boards. War rooms can be physical or virtual.

Webshops—Interactive sessions conducted over the Web.

workplace learning and performance (WLP)—The integrated use of learning and other interventions for the purpose of improving employee and organizational performance. WLP uses a systematic process of analyzing performance and responding to individual, group, and organizational needs. WLP creates positive, progressive change within organizations by balancing human, ethical, technological, and operational considerations.

Appendix C: Recommended Resources

Barksdale, Susan B., and Lund, Teri B. *Are Your Training Materials Instructionally Sound? Training and Performance Sourcebook.* Edited by Mel Silberman. New York: McGraw-Hill, 1997.

Barksdale, Susan B., and Lund, Teri B. *How to Decrease the Time Needed to Develop Performance Solutions—Training and Performance Sourcebook.* Edited by Mel Silberman. New York: McGraw-Hill, 2001.

Barksdale, Susan B., and Lund, Teri B. *How to Leverage Internal Resources—Training and Performance Sourcebook.* Edited by Mel Silberman. New York: McGraw-Hill, 2000.

Barksdale, Susan B., and Lund, Teri B. *How to Link Evaluation to the Business Need—Training and Performance Sourcebook.* Edited by Mel Silberman. New York: McGraw-Hill, 1997.

Big Dog's HR Development Page, http:wwwnwlink.com/~donclark/hrd.html.

Craig, Robert L., editor. *The ASTD Training & Development Handbook.* Alexandria, VA: ASTD, 1996.

Davidson, F. *Principles of Statistical Data Analysis.* Newbury Park, CA: Sage Publications, 1996.

Fulop, Mark F., Loop-Bartick, Kelly, and Rossett, Allison. Using the World Wide Web to Conduct a Needs Assessment. *Performance Improvement,* March 1997.

Pepitone, James S. *Future Training.* Dallas, TX: AddVantage Press, 1995.

Phillips, Jack J., and Holton, Elwood F., editors. *Conducting Needs Assessments.* Alexandria, VA: ASTD, 1995.

Robinson, Dana G., and Robinson, James C. *Training for Impact.* San Francisco: Jossey-Bass, 1989.

Rossett, Allison. Have We Overcome Obstacles to Needs Assessment? *Performance Improvement,* March 1997.

Rossett, Allison. *Using Performance Analysis in the Problem Solving Process—Training and Performance Sourcebook.* Edited by Mel Silberman. New York: McGraw-Hill, 2000.

Rothwell, William J., Sanders, Ethan S., and Soper, Jeffery G. *ASTD Models for Workplace Learning and Performance.* Alexandria, VA: ASTD, 1999.

Swanson, Richard A. *Analysis for Improving Performance.* San Francisco: Berrett-Koehler, 1994.

Woods, John A., and Cortada, James W., editors. *The 2001 ASTD Training and Performance Yearbook.* Alexandria, VA: ASTD, 2001.

About the Authors

Susan Barksdale and **Teri Lund** have a combined total of 40 years of hands-on experience in workplace learning and performance and are recognized experts in the areas of competency system development, evaluation (including how to calculate return-on-investment and how to value intellectual capital), strategic planning, needs assessment, and internal consulting. After partnering on shared projects for five years, they founded Strategic Assessment and Evaluation Associates, LLC, an entity through which they offer licensing agreements for their human performance technology models. These licensing agreements were developed in response to customer demand for the how-to behind their consulting projects. The models have proved successful in enabling clients to replicate the processes, methods, tools, and templates developed and tested by the authors over many years.

The authors are known for their practical approaches to WLP solutions and for translating complex theory into easy-to-understand applications. They have developed and implemented solutions for many organizations, including Hewlett-Packard, International Data Corporation, Intel, Microsoft, Allstate Insurance, Nike, US Bank, The Capital Group Companies, Pacificorp, and TVA.

Susan Barksdale has been a consultant to numerous large corporations for the past 12 years. Before that she managed training and consulting departments for two financial consulting firms. She holds both graduate and undergraduate degrees from the University of Wisconsin. Before entering the WLP field in 1979, she was a psychotherapist working in a major medical center and in private practice. Barksdale has taught a number of communication and behavior management courses at the University of Wisconsin-Milwaukee.

Teri Lund has been an external consultant for the past nine years. Previously she held training and performance improvement management positions for Barclays Bank, Kaiser Permanente, and Sealund and Associates. She has a bachelor of science degree in education from Montana State University and a master's degree in international business and finance from New York University. Lund has in-depth experience in implementing performance improvement strategies such as computer-based and other alternatives to delivery to classroom training, and she is a recognized leader in the area of technology and its impact on learning and performance improvement.

The Value of Belonging

ASTD membership keeps you up to date on the latest developments in your field, and provides top-quality, *actionable* information to help you stay ahead of trends, polish your skills, measure your progress, demonstrate your effectiveness, and advance your career.

We give you what you need most from the entire scope of workplace learning and performance:

Information
We're the assistants who pull together research, best practices, and background support materials – the data you need for your projects to excel.

Networking
We're the facilitator who puts you in touch with colleagues,experts, field specialists, and industry leaders – the people you need to know to succeed.

Technology
We're the clearinghouse for new technologies in training, learning, and knowledge management in the workplace – the background you need to stay ahead.

Analysis
We look at cutting-edge practices and programs and give you a balanced view of the latest tools and techniques – the understanding you need on what works and what doesn't.

Competitive Edge
ASTD is your leading resource on the issues and topics that are important to you. That's the value of belonging!

For more information, or to become a member, please call 1.800.628.2783 (U.S.) or +1.703.683.8100; visit our Website at **www.astd.org**; or send an email to customercare@astd.org.

Linking People,
Learning & Performance

859-62220